This book belongs to the great GM, Javier

Winning With the Philidor

P.s. Diego is a 🐟

Batsford Chess Library

Winning With the Philidor

Tony Kosten

An Owl Book
Henry Holt and Company
New York

Library of Congress Catalog Card Number: 92-54263

ISBN 0-8050-2428-X (An Owl Book: pbk.)

Henry Holt books are available at special discounts for
bulk purchases for sales promotions, premiums,
fund-raising, or educational use. Special editions or
book excerpts can also be created to specification.

For details contact: Special Sales Director,
Henry Holt and Company, Inc., 115 West 18th Street,
New York, New York 10011.

First American Edition—1992

Printed in the United Kingdom
Recognizing the importance of preserving the written
word, Henry Holt and Company, Inc., by policy, prints
all of its first editions on acid-free paper. ∞

10 9 8 7 6 5 4 3 2 1

Advisor: R. D. Keene GM, OBE
Technical Editor: Andrew Kinsman

Contents

Bibliography

Of the many books that I consulted whilst writing this work, the following were the most frequently consulted:

T. D. Harding, *Philidor Defense: A Reappraisal* (Chess Digest Magazine, 1974).
T. Heiling, *The Philidor Defense - Larsen Variation* (Chess Enterprises Inc. 1988).
B. Larsen (and A. Gipslis), *Why Not The Philidor Defence?* (Chess Digest Magazine, 1971).
L. M. Pickett, *Philidor Defence!?* (L. M. Pickett, 1973).
R. D. Keene, *Philidor's Defence Larsen Variation* (Modern Chess Theory).
J. Nunn, *The Complete Pirc* (B. T. Batsford, 1989).
L. Barden, W. Hartston and R. D. Keene, *The King's Indian Defence* (B. T. Batsford, 1973).
D. Bronstein, *200 Open Games* (B. T. Batsford, 1974).
Sahovski Informator Vols 1 - 50 (Chess Informant, Belgrade).
A. Matanovic, *Encyclopaedia of Chess Openings* 'C' and 'E' (*ECO*) (Chess Informant, Belgrade, 1981 and 1978).
New In Chess Vols 1 - 18 (Interchess).

Symbols

+	check	+-	White is winning
++	double check	-+	Black is winning
mate	checkmate	=	level position
!	good move	∞	unclear position
!!	excellent move	1 - 0	Black resigns
?	bad move	0 - 1	White resigns
??	blunder	½ - ½	draw agreed
!?	interesting move	Ol	olympiad
?!	dubious move	IZ	interzonal
±	small edge for White	Z	zonal
∓	small edge for Black	Ch	championship
±	clear edge for White	Corr	correspondence
∓	clear edge for Black		

Introduction

Since its heyday in the 1920s, during which time both Alekhine and Nimzowitsch employed it regularly, and despite a brief revival in the late '60s and early '70s under Larsen, the Philidor has fallen into disuse. Why is this? Why has modern opening theory decided that the last word has been written on the defence, and summarily consigned it to the scrap heap?

There are two reasons: firstly, fashion – many players are content to follow 'the latest theory' and are unwilling to have to think for themselves in the opening; and secondly, the Philidor seems to have suffered more than most defences from poor analysis and shallow generalizations.

For instance, a common criticism levelled at 2 ... d6 is that it shuts in the king's bishop, and yet if we compare it with the Ruy Lopez, the lines there in which Black brings out his king's bishop early are at best considered rather risky, whereas the main line involves Black playing ... d6 and ... ♕e7 ! How many times have I read theoreticians who say that the French Defence shuts in Black's queen's bishop? Nowadays we all know that this is an irrelevance. As to the analysis, much of the theory on Philidor's emanates from such 'up-to-date' sources as Bilguer's Handbook!

Playing the Philidor's Defence offers two main advantages: firstly, White almost invariably answers 3 d4 (whereas if you play the 'normal' 2 ... ♘c6 you have to reckon not only with the 'Spanish Torture' – 3 ♗b5 – but also with the sharp Max Lange Attack, or the Scotch Gambit, or the positional Bishop's Opening, in fact a whole host of different possibilities each requiring the memorization of a precise defence) and it is Black who chooses the battleground.

If your opponent is boring and solid, or if you want to upset a much stronger player, then you can play the ultra-sharp Mestel variation (indeed, I did just this against World Championship Candidate Sax at Hastings, and he spent over an hour pondering his first six moves!). If, on the other hand, your adversary is a sharp tactician, then why not play the solid Hanham variation and grind him down? Of course, you can always just specialize in a variation to suit your personal taste.

The second advantage is that the theory is virtually unknown.

I have played 1 e4 as a professional chess player for seven years, yet I've never bothered to look at the theory. Whenever I have encountered Philidor's Defence I have been forced to work things out myself, and not always that successfully either!

On top of that, if your opponent is acquainted with the theory, it probably won't do him much good as a lot of the established theory is mistaken anyway!

All in all, you have the opportunity to grab the psychological initiative with Black as early as move two; playing a position you understand well against an opponent who probably doesn't have a clue!

As in the other books from the 'Winning With' series, not only have I included the theory (quite a lot of it new), but also many complete games, which I have picked to illustrate important themes or strategies (or just because they are pretty!). The material is written from a Black viewpoint, but it is also, I believe, completely objective.

Unlike a lot of opening books, the reader of this book has a choice between four main, completely separate variations. I suggest that you play through the various chapters, decide on which system appeals to you most, and then learn the theory. Or why not learn all four?

As with many other openings, there is always something waiting to be discovered, and I am sure that the reader will agree: Philidor's Defence has a lot of life left in it yet.

In the words of David Bronstein: "... there can be no doubt that many of you will come to like Philidor's Defence, perhaps for ever."

1) White Third Moves other than 3 d4

1	e4	e5
2	♘f3	d6

Although in practice White almost invariably answers the Philidor's Defence with 3 d4, there are many alternatives. The only move with any real pedigree is 3 ♗c4, which was played by Steinitz and, rather more recently, by the young Kasparov, as well as being a favourite of the English Grandmaster, Murray Chandler.

This chapter, therefore, is divided into two sections:

A 3 ♗c4
B 3 Others

A

3 ♗c4

The aim of this move is to avoid the sharper lines which arise after 3 d4, and to produce a position akin to the Bishop's Opening (into which it may well transpose should Black play a later ... ♘c6).

3	...	♗e7

This is the most respectable reply; Black will content himself with simple development, adopting a formation similar to Hanham's or Antoshin's variations as circumstances permit. Black does, however, possess a number of interesting possibilities to alter the shape of the coming battle:

a) 3 ... ♘c6. This will effect a transposition into either the Hungarian Defence (if White plays d4) or Bishop's Opening (if instead White should play d3) which are both beyond the scope of this work.

b) 3 ... ♘f6!? (rather provocative) 4 ♘g5 d5 5 ed (5 ♗xd5?? ♘xd5 6 ed ♕xg5-+) 5 ... h6 (by analogy with the Two Knights Defence, 5 ... ♘xd5 cannot be recommended) 6 ♘f3 e4 7 ♘e5 ♗d6 8 ♗b5+ c6!? 9 dc 0-0 10 cb ♗xb7 with promising gambit play.

c) 3 ... c6?! 4 d4 d5 5 ed e4 (obviously 5 ... cd 6 ♗b5+ wins a pawn) 6 ♘e5 cd 7

♕h5 g6 8 ♘xg6 fg 9 ♕e5+ is better for White.

d) **3 ... ♕f6!?** (Black plans to keep the centre closed, and then launch a kingside attack with ... g5. A similar plan is possible in Hanham's variation. Certainly this could prove dangerous against a careless White player but objectively is it not correct) 4 d3 ♗g4 5 ♘bd2 ♘c6 6 c3 ♘ge7 7 h3 ♗d7 8 b4 ♘g6 9 ♘f1 ♘f4 10 ♘e3 (eyeing d5 and f5) 10 ... h6 11 ♘h2 ♕g6 12 ♕f3 ♗e7 13 h4 (intending to drive the black knight from f4 with g3) 13 ... ♗xh4!? 14 g3 ♗f6 when the game Chandler - Hodgson, Hastings 1986/7, dissolved into a tactical mess which was won by White.

e) **3 ... ♗e6!?** (this is not as bad as its reputation) 4 ♗xe6 fe 5 d4 (this is clearly the most critical reply, 5 c3 is well met by 5 ... ♘d7 6 ♕b3 ♘c5 and 5 d3 is innocuous: 5 ... ♘f6 6 c3 ♘bd7 7 0-0 ♗e7 8 ♘g5 ♘f8 9 ♕b3 ♕c8 was Borkowski - Littlewood, Mexico 1977, when 10 ♗e3 would have been slightly better for White; but 6 ... ♘c6 7 0-0 ♗e7 8 ♕b3 ♕c8 9 ♘g5 ♘d8 10 ♗e3 h6 and 11 ... 0-0 is fine for Black; if White doesn't play d4 soon Black will be able to put the f-file and the outpost on f4 to good use) 5 ... ed (5 ... ♘bd7!? may also be possible, 6 de de leaves Black with doubled, isolated pawns, but they are not on an open file, and they do control some useful central squares) 6 ♘xd4 ♘f6! (6 ... ♕d7 is a suggestion of Estrin, and may be OK, but neither 6 ... e5?! 7 ♘e6 ♕e7 8 ♕h5+ g6 9 ♕h3 ♘a6 10 ♘c3 Chandler - Large, Hastings 1986/7, the knight on e6 - which can be readily supported by f4-f5 - is like a knife in Black's throat; nor 6 ... ♕f6?! 7 ♕h5+ g6 8 ♕b5+ ♘d7 9 ♕xb7 ♖b8 10 ♕xa7 of Grob - Tartakower, Ostend 1937, is satisfactory) 7 ♘c3 (7 ♘xe6 ♕e7 8 ♘xf8 ♕xe4+ =) 7 ... ♕d7 8 0-0 e5 9 ♘de2 ♗e7 intending ... 0-0 when, according to Pachman, Black is equal. Certainly the pawn formation is good for Black, he has an extra centre pawn and the semi-open f-file.

f) **3 ... f5!?** (I like this move; now 4 d4 ed! would transpose to Mestel's variation - see chapter 3 - but to a line that I believe to be good for Black) 4 ♗xg8 ♖xg8 5 d3 ♘c6 6 ♗g5? ♗e7 is already better for Black, and 4 d3 ♘f6 5 ♗g5 h6 6 ♗xf6 ♕xf6 7 c3 ♘c6 8 b4

♗e7 9 ♘bd2 ♗e6 10 ♕b3 ♘d8 11 h3 (White is loathe to castle kingside, as Black would play ... f4 followed by ... g5 - g4, but this move is a waste of time) 11 ... 0-0 12 0-0-0?! a5 13 b5 a4 14 ♗xe6+ ♘xe6 (Black's initiative progresses nicely on both wings) 15 ♕c4 c6 16 b6 ♔h7 17 ef d5! (now the white queen is short of squares) 18 ♕g4 ♘f4 19 ♘xe5 (19 ... h5 was a big threat, trapping the queen, but this is an over-reaction) 19 ... ♕xe5 20 d4 ♕xf5 21 ♘f3 ♗a3+ and mate in two more moves N:N - Kosten, Minitel Blitz Game, 1990. White's play was not good, but this game does indicate some of Black's possibilities.

4 0-0

This would appear to be the most flexible move, 4 d3 or 4 c3 will probably transpose sooner or later, as it seems unlikely that White can do without castling altogether. The move 4 d4 is not particularly consistent here as 4 ... ed 5 ♘xd4 ♘f6 6 ♘c3 0-0 is a line from Antoshin's variation, and 5 ♕xd4 ♘f6 is Morphy's variation (chapters 6 and 7 respectively), but in both cases the bishop is probably misplaced on c4, where it serves as a target for Black's queenside play.

4 ... ♘f6
5 d3

White does have another option, namely 5 ♖e1, when 5 ... 0-0 6 ♗b3 ♘bd7 7 c3 c6 8 d3 will reach the main line although in the game Torre - Rodriguez, Black tried 7 ... ♘c5 8 ♗c2 d5?! 9 d4?! ed 10 e5 d3! (I suppose White had missed this tactical trick when he played d4, otherwise I'm sure he would have played 9 ed which wins a pawn for negligible compensation) 11 ♗xd3 ♘xd3 12 ♕xd3 ♘e4 13 c4 ♗e6 14 cd ♘c5 14 ♕e2 ♕xd5∓. As on move four, 6 d4 lets Black play a similar strategy to that of Antoshin's system. A textbook example was Mestel - Georgadze, Hastings 1979/80 (incidentally, this game commenced with the move order 1 e4 e5 2 ♗c4 d6 - Philidor's against Bishop's Opening - 3 ♘f3 ♗e7 4 0-0 ♘f6 5 ♖e1 0-0 6 d4, but although it is possible to play ... d6 against moves other than 2 ♘f3, Black must beware of White replying with 3 f4) 6 ... ed (a Hanham variation player might well prefer 6 ... ♘bd7 here, but White is not forced to reply 7 ♘c3) 7 ♘xd4 a6 8 a4 c5! 9 ♘b3 ♗e6

(Black is able to keep d5 under control) 10 ♕e2 ♘c6 11 ♘c3 (11 ♗xe6 would have only been slightly better for Black. It is remarkable how quickly White's position goes downhill from now on, despite him having only played natural moves) 11 ... ♘b4! 12 ♘d5 ♗xd5 13 ed ♖e8 14 ♖d1 ♗f8 15 ♗e3 ♖e5!∓ *(1)*

(This is the end for White's d-pawn; 16 f4 ♖xe3 17 ♕xe3 ♘xc2 wouldn't help him in the slightest) 16 ♕d2 ♘fxd5 17 ♗f4 ♘xf4 18 ♕xf4 ♕e7 and Black won easily.

| 5 | ... | 0-0 |
| 6 | c3 | c6 |

This is Black's last chance to play ... ♘c6, which would reach a standard position from Bishop's Opening, which is a little better for White. In his book, Thomas Heiling mentions the possibility 6 ... c5!?, the idea being that in comparison with the line: 6 ... ♘c6 7 ♗b3 ♘a5 8 ♗c2 c5 9 ♖e1 ♘c6, Black can save two tempi. Of course the bishop is on the less active diagonal b1-h7 here, but he does, nevertheless, have a point. Let's follow his analysis: (6 ... c5) 7 ♖e1 ♘c6 8 ♗b3 ♗g4 (8 ... ♗e6 9 ♗xe6?! fe 10 ♘g5 ♕d7 11 ♕b3 d5∞ but 9 ♘bd2 is equal) 9 ♘bd2 ♕c7, continuing ... ♖ad8, ... ♖fe8, ... ♗f8 and ... d5. This plan is worth trying.

6 ... ♗g4?! is not right here as the bishop can just serve as a target for White; 7 h3 ♗xf3? (conceding the two bishops, if 7 ... ♗h5 then White will continue 8 ♘bd2-f1-g3 and if the bishop retreats to g6 then ♘h4 will embarrass it further, but nevertheless, this would have been better) 8 ♕xf3 c6 9 ♗b3 ♘bd7 10 ♕e2 ♘c5 11 ♗c2 ♘e6 12 g3 ♕c7 13 f4! ♖fe8 14 ♘d2 ♖ad8 (Black has developed his pieces routinely, without any particular plan, and now discovers that there is nothing active he can undertake. White, on the other hand, has been steadily preparing the coming kingside onslaught) 15 ♘f3 ♔h8 16 f5 ♘f8 17 g4 h6 *(2)* 18 g5 hg 19 ♘xg5 ♔g8 20 ♔h1 ♘6h7 21 ♘f3 ♖d7 22 ♖g1 ♗d8 23 ♗h6 f6 24 ♖g2 d5 25 ♖ag1 ♖8e7 26 ed cd 27

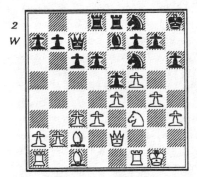

2
W

♗a4 ♖d6 28 ♖xg7+ and
wins, Steinitz - McDonnell,
Dublin 1865.

7 ♗b3 ♘bd7

This is better than 7 ...
♗e6, when the game Kas-
parov - Georgadze, USSR
Ch 1979, continued 8 ♗c2 h6
9 ♖e1 ♘bd7 10 ♘bd2 ♕c7 1
d4 ♖fe8 12 h3 ♘f8 13 c4
♘g6 14 d5 ♗d7 when Black
was being pushed back.
According to Kasparov, 11
... ♗g4 12 h3 ♗h5 13 ♘f1 ♘h7
with the plan of exchang-
ing pieces on g5, was equal.

8 ♖e1 ♘c5
9 ♗c2 ♗g4

This time this move is
associated with a real plan,
which is the use of the g5
square to exchange a
couple of pieces, thereby
easing Black's position.

10 h3 ♗h5
11 ♘bd2

11 d4 is premature: 11 ...
ed 12 cd ♘e6 13 ♗e3 d5∓ as
the knight is perfectly
placed on e6.

11 ... ♘e6

12 ♘f1 ♘e8

In the game Miklos -
Autenrieth, Budapest 1983,
Black played 12 ... ♘d7 instead and won quickly after
13 g4 (13 ♘g3 seems more
sensible, as now f4 is sen-
sitive) 13 ... ♗g6 14 ♘g3 ♘g5
15 ♔h2 ♘c5 16 ♘f5 h6 17
♘3h4 ♗f6 18 ♔g3? d5! 19 ed
cd 20 f4 ef+ 21 ♗f4 ♘ce6 22
♗xg5 ♘xg5∓.

13 ♘1h2

The point of Black's play
is revealed in the variation
13 ♘g3 ♗xf3! 14 ♕xf3 ♗g5=.

13 ... ♗g5 (3)

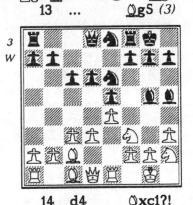

3
W

14 d4 ♗xc1?!

An innaccuracy, 14 ... ed!
15 cd ♗xc1 16 ♕xc1 d5 was
the right was to proceed,
the trade of dark-squared
bishops in this manner
would equalise.

15 ♕xc1! ed
16 ♘xd4!

The point: this knight is
no longer pinned.

16 ... ♘xd4
17 cd d5
18 ed cd

And now, instead of 19 ♖e5?!, 19 ♘b3 would have been to White's advantage. As it was, the game Psakhis – Tseshkovsky, USSR Ch 1980/1 soon terminated in a draw.

Although 3 ... ♗e7 is Black's most solid reply to 3 ♗c4, it is evident from the large choice of other third moves for Black offering the second player a good game, that 3 ♗c4 should present him with few problems.

B Other White third moves

1   e4   e5
2   ♘f3   d6

At this juncture White has a very large choice of moves; by and large, he has preferred to play the aggressive 3 d4 or 3 ♗c4. It is difficult to give any hard or fast rules to follow should one's adversary play anything unusual, I myself prefer to either adopt a Pirc-type set-up with ... g6 and ... ♗g7, or to react with ... f5. This is a matter of taste as much as anything else, and it is just as good to play, say, a Hanham formation instead.

Anyway, below is a brief selection of possibilities:

a) **3 ♗e2** ♘f6 4 ♘c3 c6 (4 ... g6 must also be good) 5 d4 ♕c7 6 a4 ♗e7 7 a5 0-0 8 0-0 ♗g4 (8 ... ♘bd7 would lead directly to a Hanham type formation, Black's move is more ambitious) 9 ♗e3 ♘bd7 10 ♘h4?!, Kindermann – Gross, Stary Smokovec 1987 (by transposition) and now 10 ... ♘xe4! 11 ♗xg4 ♘xc3 12 bc ♗xh4 was unclear.

b) **3 ♘c3** is a flexible move, and Black probably does best to play 3 ... ♘f6 which, after 4 d4, will transpose into one of the main lines considered in this book. If instead 3 ... f5 then 4 d4 is variation C of chapter 3, and 3 ... ♘c6 4 ♗b5 is a Ruy Lopez.

c) **3 c3** (aiming to set up a strong centre with d4, but Black is well placed to meet this) 3 ... f5! 4 ♗c4 (4 ef ♗xf5 5 ♕b3 ♘f6 6 ♘g5 d5 7 ♕xb7 ♘bd7 8 ♕c6 ♗d6, Lepeshkin – Terpugov, USSR 1959, when Black's centre and lead in development are more than enough compensation for the pawn) 4 ... ♘f6 5 d4 fe 6 de ef 7 ef ♕xf6 8 gf ♘c6 9 f4 ♗d7 10 ♗e3 0-0-0 11 ♘d2 ♖e8 12 ♕f3 ♗f5 13 0-0-0? d5! 14 ♗xd5 *(4)*

14 ... ♕xc3+! 15 bc ♗a3 mate 0-1, Schulder – Boden, circa 1865. They don't play chess like that anymore!

d) **3 c4** g6 (3 ... f5, similar

to the above, also seems to be strong) 4 ♘c3 ♗g7 5 d3 (5 d4 is more to the point, 5 ... ed would then be Larsen's variation) 5 ... ♘e7 6 ♗e3 ♘bc6 7 ♕d2 ♘d4 8 ♗xd4 ed 9 ♘e2 c5 10 h3 0-0 (already ∓) 11 b4 f5 12 ♘g3 cb 13 ♕xb4 ♘c6 14 ♕d2 fe 15 ♘xe4 ♗f5 16 ♗e2 ♗xe4 and ... d3 winning, N.N.-Kosten, Minitel Blitz game 1990.

e) **3 d3** g6 4 ♗e2 ♗g7 5 0-0 ♘f6 6 ♘c3 0-0 7 h3 ♘c6

8 ♖e1 h6 9 ♗f1 (White decides that he likes the look of Black's fianchetto and so copies it; however, he is now behind in development) 9 ... ♗e6 10 g3 d5 11 ♗g2 ♕d7 12 ♔h2 ♖ad8 13 ♕e2 ♖fe8 14 b3 ♘d4 15 ♘xd4 ed 16 ♘a4 de 17 a3 b6 18 ♗b2 c5∓ *(5)*

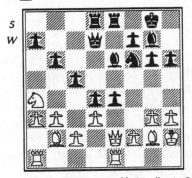

19 de ♗d5 20 ♕d3 ♗c6 21 ♖e2? ♗b5 and Black won easily, 'Blac' - Kosten, Minitel Blitz game 1991.

2) Unusual Black replies to 3 d4

1	e4	e5
2	♘f3	d6
3	d4	

I don't intend to dwell long on these moves as they all lead to an inferior, or perhaps even lost, position for Black. From the point of view of *Winning With the Philidor* these moves are I'm afraid, real non-starters.

Having said that, however, there are two interesting lines involving the sacrifice of a pawn that, whilst not being completely sound, might well prove successful in blitz or semi-rapid games.

So we have

A 3 ... ♘d7
B 3 ... ♗g4
C 3 ... ♗d7

A

| | 3 | ... | ♘d7 |

This is the original Hanham variation. Many of the classic Hanham games commenced with this move order, but, unfortunately, there is a tactical flaw, involving an early ♗c4 and ♘g5, that renders this line almost unplayable.

It is more for this reason that Hanham's system is nowadays introduced only after the preliminary 3 ... ♘f6 4 ♘c3 and now 4 ... ♘bd7 when after 5 ♗c4 ♗e7 any sorties of the white king's knight to g5 can be met by the simple ... 0-0.

| | 4 | ♗c4 |

Obviously there are alternatives to this move, but they are not critical and will probably transpose to lines considered in chapter 8.

| | 4 | ... | c6 |

A necessary precaution. The immediate 4 ... ♗e7 loses a pawn to 5 de ♘xe5 (5 ... de?? is even worse, 6 ♕d5±) 6 ♘xe5 de 7 ♕h5 g6 8 ♕xe5 and whilst 4 ... h6 has the merit of stopping ♘g5, it does permit 5 de de (5 ... ♘xe5 6 ♘xe5 de 7 ♗xf7+ is disastrous for Black) 6 ♗xf7+ ♔xf7 7 ♘xe5+ ♔f6 8 ♕d4! c5 (the only sensible move that I can see) 9 ♘xd7++ ♔e7 10 ♕xc5+ ♔xd7 11 ♕b5+ with a strong attack and three pawns for the piece. 4 ... ♘gf6 5 de ♘xe5 6 ♘xe5 de 7 ♗xf7+ ♔xf7 8 ♕xd8 ♗b4+ 9 ♕d2 ♗xd2+ 10 ♘xd2 also wins a pawn for White.

5 0-0

This seems the most natural move, yet White also gets a strong position after both **5 de** de 6 ♘g5 ♘h6 7 0-0 ♗e7 8 ♘e6 fe 9 ♗xh6 ♘b6 10 ♕h5+ ♔f8 11 f4 ♗c5+ 12 ♔h1 ♔g8 13 f5 gh 14 fe ♕e7 15 ♖f7 ♕g5 16 ♖f8+! *(6)*

and mate next move, 1-0, (Van der Wiel - Van Baarle, Amsterdam 1983), and **5 ♘c3** ♗e7 (5 ... h6 is often given as bad on the basis of Unzicker - Blau, Lucerne 1948, which continued: 6 a4 ♕f6?! 7 h4 g6 8 ♗e3 with advantage to White, but, by analogy with a previous variation, why not continue with 6 de de 7 ♗xf7+ ♔xf7 8 ♘xe5+ ♔e6 9 ♘g6, when the

Black king's prospects seems very poor?) 6 de de (6 ... ♘xe5? 7 ♘xe5 de 8 ♕h5 g6 9 ♕xe5+- occurred in an early game of Fischer's, against Goldsmith, USA 1957) 7 ♘g5 ♗xg5 (7 ... ♘h6 is no improvement; 8 ♘e6! fe 9 ♗xh6 ♘b6 10 ♕h5+ ♔f8 11 ♗b3 gh 12 ♖d1 followed by ♕xh6+ and ♖d3-f3 is devastating) 8 ♕h5 g6 (8 ... ♕f6 9 ♗xg5 ♕g6 10 ♕h4 also leads to a large advantage for White, Schlechter - Alekhine, Hamburg 1910) 9 ♕xg5 ♕xg5 10 ♗xg5 with a fairly typical endgame for this variation. The game Tal - Menvielle, Spain 1966, continued 10 ... ♘f8 11 0-0-0 ♗e6 12 ♗e2 (naturally, White wishes to retain both of his bishops) 12 ... ♘d7 13 ♖d6 ♘e7 14 ♖hd1; and the correspondence game Salonen - Batik 1976, featured the 'improvement' 10 ... ♘c5, when 11 0-0-0 ♗e6 12 ♗e2 f6 13 ♗e3 ♘d7 14 ♖d6 ♔e7 15 ♖hd1 ♘f8 16 ♗c5 ♔e8 17 ♘b5! *(7)*

17 ... cb 18 ♖xe6+! ♔f7 was easily winning for White, 18 ... ♘xe6 being met by 19 ♗xb5+ ♔f7 20 ♖d7+, regaining the sacrificed material with a hefty premium. In both cases the two bishops and Black's weakness on the dark squares was just

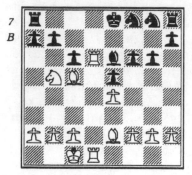

too much to bear.

     5 ...   ♗e7

5 ... h6 is even worse in this position, as 6 de de 7 ♗xf7+ ♔xf7 8 ♘xe5+ ♔f6 9 ♕f3+! led to a king-hunt in the game Georgiev - Pelitov, Bulgaria 1974: 9 ... ♔xe5 10 ♕f7 ♘gf6 11 ♖d1 ♗c5 12 ♘d2 and the end was in sight; 5 ... ♕c7 6 ♘g5 ♘h6 7 f4 is no better.

     6 de   de

Again, 6 ... ♘xe5? 7 ♘xe5 de 8 ♕h5 acquires a pawn.

     7 ♘g5   ♗xg5

The attentive reader will have noticed by now that 7 ... ♘h6 loses rather quickly to 8 ♘e6! fe 9 ♗xh6 ♘b6 10 ♕h5+ g6 (10 ... ♔f8 11 f4+-) 11 ♕e2 ♘xc4 12 ♕xc4 ♕c7 13 ♘d2; the black kingside is full of holes, and his queen's bishop is a miserable piece.

     8 ♕h5   ♕e7

Both 8 ... g6 9 ♕xg5 ♕xg5 10 ♗xg5 ♘c5 (10 ... h6 11 ♗d2 g5 12 ♗c3 Steiner - Brinckmann, Budapest 1929) 11

♘d2 ♗e6 12 ♗e2! (White learnt well from his game against Tal) 12 ... f6 13 ♗e3 ♘d7 14 a4 ♘e7 15 ♘c4 followed by doubling the rooks on the d-file, and winning not long after, Menvielle - Garcia, Arrecife 1973, and 8 ... ♕f6 9 ♗xg5 ♕g6 10 ♕h4 are also witnesses to White's advantage.

     9 ♕xg5

9 ♗xg5 is also very good: 9 ... ♘gf6 10 ♕e2 (10 ♕h4 h6 11 ♘c3 ♖h7 12 ♗xf6 ♘xf6 13 ♖ad1± Butnoris - Bastrikov, USSR 1968) 10 ... h6 11 ♗d2 0-0 12 a4 b6 13 f3 ♗b7 14 ♗e3 a6 15 ♕f2, Gipslis - Csom, Budapest 1977, White enjoying a considerable advantage, which he managed to convert into a point some thirty-two moves later. The text is perhaps more logical in that the advantage of the bishop pair will be more marked in the endgame.

	9 ...	♕xg5
	10 ♗xg5	♘gf6
	11 f3	♘c5
	12 ♘d2	♘fd7

In view of what follows, 12 ... a5 is better, but Black's position would still be clearly worse.

     13 b4!

White begins a general advance on the queenside which will rapidly squash

Black. It is typical of the bishop-pair that they facilitate pawn rolls of this type, and it is also fairly common to see the knights both running out of meaningful squares at the same time.

| 13 | ... | ♘a4 |

If Black had tried 13 ... ♘e6 instead then 14 ♗xe6 fe 15 ♘c4 wuld be clearly advantageous for White, opposite coloured bishops notwithstanding.

14	♗b3	♘ab6
15	c4	f6
16	♗e3	♘f8
17	c5	♘bd7
18	♘c4	♔e7 (8)

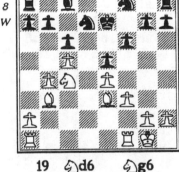

19	♘d6	♘g6
20	♘f5+	♔f8
21	♖fd1	♘f4

The knight is not allowed to rest here for long; White rapidly wins a piece and with it the game.

22	g3	♘h3+
23	♔g2	♘g5
24	♗xg5!	fg
25	♗e6	g6

| 26 | ♘d6 | ♘b6 |
| 27 | ♗b3 | 1-0 |

A textbook display! (Dreev - Korhonen, Kiljava Jnr Ch 1984)

B

| 3 | ... | ♗g4 |

One of the most famous games ever played with Philidor's Defence featured this third move. The game in question was between Paul Morphy (who had the white pieces) and the Duke of Brunswick and Count Isouard (who shared the black pieces) and the move 3 ... ♗g4 never recovered from the mauling it received at the hands of the young American.

The game went as follows:

| 4 | de | ♗xf3? |

In the contemporary analysis of this game, this is given as being forced, else Black will lose a pawn (4 ... de? 5 ♕xd8+ ♔xd8 6 ♘xe5). However, as Black is also clearly worse after the text move, then from Black's point of view we should examine the alternatives:

There are two other moves: firstly 4 ... ♘c6!? which invites White to grab a pawn by 5 ed ♗xd6, when Black will continue with ... ♕d7 (... ♕e7) and ... 0-0-0, Black will have a lead in development and free play for his pieces as compensation for the pawn. I seem to remember that the English Grandmaster, Julian Hodgson used to play this gambit with some success when he was very, very young. The main drawback is that White can prefer 5 ♗b5, when 5 ... de 6 ♕xd8+ ♖xd8 7 ♗xc6+ bc 8 ♗e3 (8 ♘xe5?? ♖d1 mate) 8 ... ♗d6 9 ♘bd2 leaves White with a nagging endgame advantage, although Black does have the two bishops to console him. Secondly, we have **4 ... ♘d7?!**, which as 5 ♗b5 is no longer a sensible possibility, forces White to accept the pawn offer (although in the game Pollock – Blackburne, Hastings 1895, White did play the rather limp 5 ♗e2?!) and 5 ed ♗xd6 6 ♗e2 ♕e7 7 0-0 0-0-0 reaches a position where Black, again, has something in return for his pawn, although his queen's knight is less actively placed. As I mentioned at the start, both these moves are often worth a try, if only in off-hand games.

    5   ♕xf3

Maroczy mentions that 5 gf de 6 ♕xd8+ ♔xd8 7 f4 is good for White, but I would be tempted to try 5 ... ♘c6!, wouldn't you?

5	...	de
6	♗c4	♘f6?

6 ... ♕d7 is a better try.

7	♕b3	♕e7
8	♘c3!	

Morphy spurns the win of the b-pawn, as after 8 ♕xb7 ♕b4+ Black will be able to fight on a bit. It would seem that he was in a hurry to finish!

8	...	c6
9	♗g5	b5?
10	♘xb5!	cb
11	♗xb5+	♘bd7
12	0-0-0	♖d8
13	♖xd7!	♖xd7
14	♖d1	♕e6

Now 15 ♗xf6 ♕xb3 16 ♗xd7 mate is convincing, but Morphy chooses a more aesthetic route.

15	♗xd7+	♘xd7
16	♕b8+!	♘xb8
17	♖d8 mate	*(9)* 1-0

This was played in Paris, 1858.

C

3	...	♗d7?!

Yet another gambit variation. The idea, as before, is to develop the queenside pieces as quickly as possible and play castles long, without allowing an inconvenient ♗b5. The one example I have was most encouraging for Black: 4 de ♘c6 5 ed ♗xd6 6 ♗c4 ♕e7 7 ♗e3 0-0-0 8 ♘bd2 ♗g4 9 c3 ♘f6 10 ♕c2 ♗c5 11 ♗f4? ♗xf3 12 gf ♘h5 13 ♗g3 f5! with a crushing position, Kubler - Lilienthal, Corr. Of course, White's play was hopeless, but it does show the kind of initiative that Black can get in these gambit systems if White is not on his guard.

3) Mestel's Variation

This system is also known as Philidor's Counter-attack, but as the entire variation bears Philidor's name, I have taken the liberty of renaming it after the English Grandmaster, Jonathan Mestel, who took this little known system out of moth-balls in the seventies and scored a number of fine wins with it.

1	e4	e5
2	♘f3	d6
3	d4	f5!? *(10)*

Essentially, there are four 'refutations'.

A 4 de
B 4 ♗c4
C 4 ♘c3

D 4 ef

A

4 de

The most popular and most forcing line.

| 4 | ... | fe |
| 5 | ♘g5 | |

Obviously, 5 ♗g5 ♗e7 6 ♗xe7 ♘xe7 7 ♘g5 d5 8 e6 0-0 9 ♕h5 (or 9 ♘f7 ♕e8 10 ♕g4 ♘g6) 9 ... h6 only favours Black, who has a lead in development and also (a recurring theme in this system) an extra central pawn.

| 5 | ... | d5 |
| 6 | e6! | |

Driving a wedge into the black position. The game van der Sterren – Mestel, Tjentishte 1975, developed differently: **6 c4!?** ♗b4+ 7 ♘c3 (7 ♗d2 ♕xg5 8 ♗xb4 dc is good for Black – Mestel) 7 ... d4 8 a3 ♗xc3+ 9 bc e3!? (9 ... ♘c6 10 ♘xe4 ♕h4 may be better, according to Mestel, but who wouldn't want this black pawn chain?) 10 f4 c5 11 ♗d3 ♘e7 12 0-0 (both 12 ♘xh7 ♖xh7 and 12 ♗xh7 ♖xh7 are very unclear) 12 ... ♘bc6 13 ♘e4? (possibly 13 e6 ♕d6 is better) *(11)*

13 ... 0-0 14 ♘xc5 ♘f5 15 ♘b3? (White finally manages to break up the black pawns, but a the cost of a lost ending) 15 ... dc 16 ♗xf5 ♕xd1 17 ♖xd1 ♗xf5 18 ♗xe3 ♗c2 19 ♘c5 ♗xd1 20 ♖xd1 ♘a5! 21 ♖d3 ♘xc4 22 ♗c1 ♖ac8 23 ♘xb7 c2, winning easily. The move 6 ♘c3 was suggested by Steinitz, 6 ... c6 7 e6 will transpose, but 6 ... ♗b4!? might be playable, e.g. 7 a3 ♗xc3+ 8 bc ♘e7 or 7 e6 ♕f6∞.

The strange **6 h4!?** is fairly typical of the sort of rubbish weaker players have tried against me in quick games. One of my games from the Franconville Semi-Rapid tournament 1991 continued: 6 ... ♘c6 7 ♗f4 ♗b4+ 8 c3 ♗c5 9 e6 ♕f6 10 ♕g4 ♘h6 (meeting 11 ♕h5+ with 11 ... g6 12 ♕xh6 ♕xf4-+ of course) 11

♕g3 0-0 when White was already lost.

6 ... ♘h6

This is the most obvious, guarding against ♘f7, but Black has three other possibilities.

a) 6 ... ♗c5?! 7 ♘c3 (7 ♘xe4! is probably also good, 7 ... ♕e7. Not 7 ... de? 8 ♕h5+ g6 9 ♕xc5±. *8 ♕g4!?* 8 ♘g5!? might be better, compare with Sax - Kosten in (b). *8 ... g6 9 ♘g5 ♘h6 10 ♕h4 ♘f5 11 ♕a4+ c6 12 ♘f7 ♕b6 13 ♘xh8 ♗c5*. This might be an error, as 14 ♘f7!? might be good, withdrawing the knight - 13 ... *♗xe6!*. *14 ♕f4? ♗xe6 15 ♘c3 ♗d6 16 ♕g5 ♗e7*, Rosenthal - Pitschel, Paris 1878, when Black will have a little compensation for the exchange when he manages to recapture the knight. The more blatant *7 ♘f7?* is a mistake, however, and was convincingly refuted in the game Barnes - Morphy, London 1858: 7 ... *♕f6 8 ♗e3 d4 9 ♗g5 ♕f5 10 ♘xh8 ♕xg5 11 ♗c4 ♘c6 12 ♘f7 ♕xg2 13 ♖f1 ♘f6 14 f3? ♘b4! (12)*

15 ♘a3 ♗xe6 16 ♗xe6 ♘d3+ 17 ♕xd3 ed 18 0-0-0 ♗xa3 19 ♗b3 d2+ 20 ♔b1 ♗c5 21 ♘e5 ♔f8 22 ♘d3 ♖e8! 23 ♘xc5 ♕xf1! 24 ♘e6+ ♖xe6 0-1) 7 ... c6 (7 ... *♕f6* is simply answered by 8 ♘gxe4 ♕xe6

9 ♕xd5±) 8 ♘f7 ♕f6 9 ♗e3
d4? (Black would have
reasonable compensation
for the exchange after 9 ...
♗xe3! 10 fe ♗xe6 11 ♘xh8 g6
or 11 ... ♕h4+ 12 g3 ♕h6) 10
♕h5! (10 ♘cxe4 is not bad
either) 10 ... de 11 ♘d6++
♔d8 12 ♕e8+ ♔c7 13 ♕xc8+
♔xd6 14 ♘xe4+.

b) 6 ... ♗b4+?! (the idea is
to play variation 'a' without
the possibility of 7 ♘c3) 7
c3 ♗c5 8 ♘xe4! (8 ♘f7 is
not so convincing; 8 ... ♕f6
9 ♗e3 ♗xe6 10 ♘xh8 ♗xe3 11
fe ♕h4+ 12 g3 ♕h6 13 ♕d2
♘d7 14 c4 - or 14 ♕f2 ♘e7
15 ♕f4 ♕xf4 16 gf 0-0-0
and ... ♖xh8 - 14 ... ♘e5 15
♗e2 dc 16 ♘c3 ♘d3+ 17 ♗xd3
ed (13)
Analysis by Meckarov, with
play for the exchange, assuming the knight on h8 is
captured) 8 ... ♗e7 9 ♘g5!
(when I originally wrote
the rough draft for this
chapter, I thought that 6 ...
♗b4+ was Black's strongest
move, so so I decided to try

it against one of the finest
tacticians in the world, Gy-
ula Sax, by way of experi-
ment. As I mentioned in
the introduction, he spent
over one hour on his first
few moves, but then, un-
fortunately, found the move
9 ♘g5 which appears to
assure White the advant-
age. 9 ♕g4!? is also possible. I analysed: 9 ... g6 10
♘g5 ♘h6 11 ♕h4 - 11 ♕a4+?
♘c6 12 ♘f7 ♘xf7 13 ef+
♔xf7∓ - 11 ... ♘f5 12 ♕a4+
c6 13 ♘f7 ♕b6 14 ♘xh8 -
this is similar to the Rosenthal - Pitschel game -
14 ... ♗xe6! 15 ♗e2 ♘d7 16
0-0 0-0-0 17 ♘xg6?! hg 18
♘d2 ♘c5 19 ♕c2 d4 with the
initiative) 9 ... ♗xg5 (a difficult decision to have to
make, but 9 ... ♕d6 10 ♕h5+
g6 11 ♕e2 ♘h6 12 h4 is also
unpleasant) 10 ♕h5+ g6 11
♕xg5 ♕xg5 (or 11 ... ♗xe6 12
♕e5 ♕f6 13 ♕xc7± or 11 ...
♕d6 12 ♗f4 ♕xe6+ 13 ♕e5;
finally 11 ... ♘f6 12 ♗d3 0-0
13 ♗xg6!? or 13 0-0 with the

idea of ♕h4, ♗h6 etc) 12 ♗xg5 ♗xe6? (I had pinned too much faith on a dis-covered check, 12 ... c6 was the only chance, but it is slightly better for White because of the two bish-ops) 13 ♗f4 ♘c6 (14 ♗e5 was the threat) 14 ♗xc7 ♔d7 15 ♗f4 ♖e8 *(14)*

16 ♘a3! ♗g4+ 17 ♔d2 ♘f6 18 f3 ♗e6 19 ♘b5 and Black was completely lost, al-though I tried to set a couple of tricks! Sax – Kosten, Hastings 1990/1.

c) **6 ... ♘f6!?** an idea of Meckarov's, 7 ♘f7 ♕e7 8 ♘xh8 ♗xe6∞. As in all these variation, if Black can regain the piece on h8 without losing any time then his strong centre will provide good compensation for the exchange.

7 ♘c3! c6

Forced. 7 ... ♗b4?? 8 ♕h5+ g6 9 ♕xh6+-.

8 ♘gxe4!

This has been known to be the best move since the eighteenth century! 8 ♘xh7? (with the idea of 8 ... ♖xh7? 9 ♕h5+ ♔e7 10 ♗g5+±) re-bounds: 8 ... ♗xe6! 9 ♘xf8 ♗f7! 10 ♗e3 ♖xf8 11 ♕d4 ♖g8 12 0-0-0 ♘d7 13 ♕d2 (... c5 and ... d4 was threat-ened) 13 ... ♘g4 *(15)*

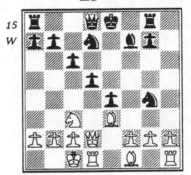

(13 ... ♘f5 looks to be even better to me) and Black's strong centre gives him a considerable advantage. Spasskov - Pishkov, Bul-garia Ch 1965. Other moves would allow Black to con-solidate with ... ♕f6, ... ♗c5 etc.

8 ... de?!

Acceptance of the piece sacrifice might lose. Black has an interesting alterna-tive in 8 ... ♘f5!? 9 ♘g5 ♕f6 10 ♗d3 h6 (10 ... ♗xe6 looks OK as well, 11 ♘xe6 ♕xe6+ 12 ♕e2 ♕xe2+ leaves White with the bishop pair in the endgame, but Black's strong centre offers him level chances. Alternatively, 11 0-0 ♗d7! 12 ♖e1+ ♗e7 13 ♕e2 0-0! 14 ♗xf5? ♕xf5 15

♕xe7?? ♕xf2+ 16 ♔h1 ♕f1+ and mate next move. This line needs tests) 11 ♕f3 g6 12 g4! (12 ♘h3 is nothing: 12 ... ♗g7 intending ... 0-0, ... ♗xe6, ... ♘d4) 12 ... hg 13 gf ♗b4!? (I suppose other bishop moves may be possible, but not 13 ... ♗xe6? 14 ♗xg5! ♕xg5 - 14 ... ♕f7?? 15 fe ♕xf3 16 ♗xg6++- - 15 fe with the advantage) 14 ♘d2 *(16)*

An interesting position for analysis, 14 ... ♗xe6! 15 ♗xg5 (15 0-0-0 gf or ♗xf5 should be good for Black) 15 ... ♗xc3+ (15 ... ♕xg5 16 fe ♖f8 17 ♕g3) 16 bc ♕xc3+ 17 ♔e2 gf and I think that this should be fine for Black, e.g: 18 ♕e3 ♔f7 19 ♗f4 ♘d7 with ... ♖ae8 and ... d4 to come.

>   9   ♕h5+   g6
> 10   ♕e5   ♖g8
> 11   ♗g5!

This is better than 11 ♗xh6 ♗xh6 12 ♖d1 ♕g5! (the most active, 12 ... ♕e7? 13 ♗c4 b5 14 ♗b3 a5? - 14 ...

♗g7 was a better chance - 15 ♘xe4! a4 16 ♘f6+ ♔f8 17 ♘xg8 ♔xg8 *(17)*

18 ♖d8+! ♕xd8 19 e7+ 1-0, Atwood - Wilson, London 1798. Incidentally, the players were both contemporaries of Philidor, although he could give them considerable odds) 13 ♕c7 ♗xe6 14 ♕xb7 e3! *(18)* (typical Morphy! The menace is ... ef+ and then ... ♕e3 mate).

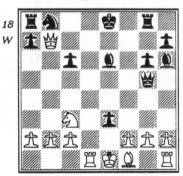

15 f3 ♕e7 16 ♕xa8 ♔f7 (trapping the white queen) 17 ♘e4 ♗f4 18 ♗e2 ♔g7 19 0-0 ♕c7 20 ♘c5 (else 20 ... ♘d7 wins White's queen) 20 ... ♗xh2+ 21 ♔h1 ♗c8 22 ♖d4 ♗g3 23 ♕e4 ♔h8! 24

♖d1 ♕g7! 25 ♖h4 (the only way to stop ... ♕h6+. The players of the white pieces try their utmost to save the game) 25 ... ♗xh4 26 ♕xb8 ♗a6 27 ♕h2 ♗xe2 28 ♖d7 ♕h6 29 ♘e4 ♗c4 30 ♘f6 e2 31 ♖e7 ♕c1+ 32 ♕g1 ♕xg1+ 33 ♔xg1 e1(♕)+ 34 ♖xe1 ♗xe1 0-1. A tough battle! Staunton and Owen – Morphy and Barnes, London 1858.

11 ... ♗g7

11 ... ♕d6? 12 ♖d1 ♕xe6 13 ♗c4!±.

12 e7 ♕d7?!

This looks like an ugly move to have to play, and is 12 ... ♕b6!? 13 0-0-0 ♘d7 (or even 13 ... ♗d7) so awful? For example, 14 ♕f4 ♘f5 15 ♗c4 (the queen's knight is unable to participate, 15 ♘xe4? ♕xb2+) 15 ... h6!? 16 ♗xg8 hg 17 ♕xe4 ♘xe7 18 ♖he1 ♘e5∓; or 14 ♕xe4 (or 14 ♕e6) 14 ... ♘f7. The position is so complicated that I would not like to put money on any of these variations. It's at times like these that I think it would be nice to borrow 'Deep Thought' for a couple of days to work it all out!

13 ♕f4 ♕f5

13 ... ♘f5 14 ♖d1 ♕e6 15 ♖d8+ ♔f7 16 ♖xg8 ♔xg8 17 ♗c4 fares no better – Sozin.

14 ♗xh6 ♗e6
15 0-0-0 ♕xf4+

16 ♗xf4 ♗xc3
17 ♗g5 ♘d7
18 bc

And White is winning – Berger.

However, I think I have shown that things are not at all clear, and further I believe that there are other improvements to be found; all that is required are practical tests in tournaments.

B

4 ♗c4 ed!

Other moves are patently inferior:

a) **4 ... fe?** 5 ♘xe5 d5 (5 ... de 6 ♕h5+ ♔d7 7 ♕f5+ ♔c6 8 ♕xe5 – better than 8 ♕xe4+, Bronstein – Saadi, Cordova 1968 – 8 ... a6 – 8 ... ♘f6? hastens the end; 9 ♕b5+ ♔d6 10 ♗f4+ ♔e7 11 ♕e5+ ♔d7 12 ♕e6 mate Diepstraaten – Zschorn, Corr – 9 d5+ ♔b6 10 ♗e3+ with a winning attack) 6 ♕h5+ g6 7 ♘xg6 ♘f6 8 ♕e5+ ♗e7 and now either 9 ♘xh8 dc 10 ♘c3 ♘c6 11 ♕g5 ♗e6 12 0-0 ♕d7 13 d5 ♘xd5 14 ♕h5+ – Steinitz; or the simpler 9 ♗b5+ c6 10 ♘xe7 ♕xe7 11 ♕xe7+ ♔xe7 12 ♗e2 ♖g8 13 g3 – analysis by Keres – are advantageous for White.

b) **4 ... ♘f6** 5 ♘g5 ♕e7 (5 ... d5 is even worse; 6 de de 7 ♕xd8+ ♔xd8 8 ef, menacing ♘f7+) 6 ♗f7+ ♔d8 7

♗b3 ed 8 0-0±.

c) **4 ... ♘c6!?** is an idea of Morphy's. Now 5 de fe 6 ♘g5 ♘xe5 7 ♗d5 seems fine for Black but, nevertheless, the well-tested main line is strongly recommended.

5 ♘g5

Obviously 5 ♕xd4 ♘c6 or 5 ♘xd4 fe 6 ♕h5+ (6 ♘c3 ♘f6 with the intention of continuing ... d5 or ... c6 and ... d5∓) 6 ... g6 7 ♕d5 ♕e7 8 ♗g5 ♘f6 9 ♗xf6 (forced, 9 ♕b5+? c6 10 ♕b3 d5∓) 9 ... ♕xf6 10 ♕xe4+ ♕e7 11 ♘e6 (11 ♕xe7+ ♗xe7∓ - two bishops) 11 ... ♗xe6 12 ♕xe6 ♕xe6 13 ♗xe6 ♘c6 14 c3 ♔e7 15 ♗b3 ♗g7= offer nothing for White, and (5 ♘xd4 fe) 6 ♗xg8 ♖xg8 7 ♕h5+ g6 8 ♕xh7 ♖g7 9 ♕h8 c5! 10 ♗h6? ♖f7 11 ♘b3 ♕h4 12 ♗g7 ♕f4 is a positive catastrophe. Finally; 5 ef d5 6 ♗d3 ♕e7+ 7 ♗e2 ♗xf5 8 ♘xd4 ♗g4 9 f3 ♗d7 10 0-0 ♘c6 11 ♖e1 0-0-0! 12 ♘c3 ♕h4 13 ♘xc6?! ♗c5+ and Black won, Keller - Mestel, Bern 1975.

5 ... ♘h6
6 0-0

6 ♘xh7 (with the idea 6 ... ♖xh7? 7 ♕h5+ ♔d7 8 ♕g6±) was once considered to be a refutation of this system, that is, until the game Nurmi - Mestel, Tjentishte 1975: 6 ... ♘g4! 7 ♘xf8 (7 ♘g5 ♕f6! 8 ♘f7

♖h5 traps the errant knight, 8 ♗f7+ ♔e7! and 8 c3 ♘c6! are also good for Black) 7 ... ♔xf8 8 ef?! (8 ♕xd4 might be better, but 8 ... ♘c6 9 ♕d5 ♘ce5 10 ♗b3 c6 11 ♕d4 ♘xh2 is extremely awkward for White, as ... ♘ (either) f3 is threatened) 8 ... ♕e7+ 9 ♔f1 (the endgame is very pleasant for Black with his two extra centre pawns) 9 ... ♗xf5 10 ♕xd4 ♘xh2+ 11 ♖xh2 ♖xh2 12 ♗e3 *(19)*

12 ... ♕e4 (Black, now an exchange to the good, elects to play the ending) 13 ♕xe4 ♖h1+! 14 ♔e2 ♗xe4 0-1 "Note the extra centre pawn" - Mestel.

6 ... ♘c6
7 ♖e1

This is the latest attempt at refutation, 7 ef ♗xf5 8 ♖e1+ ♔d7 9 c3 (perhaps *9 ♗e6+ ♗xe6 10 ♘xe6 ♕h4=* was better, but White must still be careful, e.g.: *11 ♗g5 ♕g4 12 f3 ♕f5 13 ♗xh6 gh 14 ♘xd4 ♕c5 15 c3 ♗g7∓*. However, the enticing-looking *9 ♘e6?* seems to rebound, i.e. *9 ... ♕f6 10 ♗g5 ♕g6 11 ♕e2 ♖e8 12 ♗xh6 gh.* Obviously not *12 ... ♕xh6?? 13 ♘c5+. 13 ♘xf8+ ♖hxf8 14 ♕d2 ♗h3 15 ♗f1 ♗xg2! 16 ♗xg2 ♖g8* with win of material and mate to follow, 'Ljubo' - Kosten, Minitel 1991) *9 ... ♕f6 10 ♕b3 ♗e7 11 ♘e6 ♖ab8 12 cd ♕h4 13 ♘xg7 ♘xd4 14 ♘xf5 ♘hxf5 15 ♗e6+ ♔d8∓ (20)*

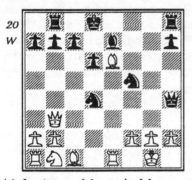

(Adorjan - Mestel, Moscow 1977) *16 ♕d3 ♘xe6 17 ♖xe6 (17 ♕xf5? ♖f8∓) 17 ... ♕d4 18 ♕b3 ♖f8* or *17 ... ♖f8.* The white attack may appear dangerous but, in reality, he has yet to develop his queenside and Black's king can hide safely behind his centre pawns.

7 ... f4!

Black must keep the e-file closed, *7 ... fe? 8 ♘xe4 ♘e5 9 ♗xh6 gh 10 f4 ♘c4 11 ♘xd6+±.* As he has a pawn more, Black can afford to return it.

8 ♗xf4 ♕f6
9 ♕d2 ♘e5

Meckarov suggests *9 ... ♗e7!?*, but I prefer the text.

10 ♗e2 ♗e7!

This is my improvement, taking advantage of the looseness of White's king-side pieces. *10 ... ♗g4? 11 f3 ♗d7 12 ♗g3 0-0-0 13 f4±* of Parjalis - Arhipkin, USSR 1978 was all wrong.

11 ♘f3

11 ♘a3? 0-0 12 g3 ♘g6∓ or *12 ♗xe5 de 13 ♘f3∓.*

11 ... ♘xf3+
12 ♗xf3 ♘f7!∓

Black menaces ... 0-0 and ... ♘e5, or even, in some cases, ... g5 and ... h5 catching a bishop. For example, *13 ♘a3 ♗d7 14 ♖ad1 (14 ♘c4 ♘e5) 14 ... 0-0 15 ♗g3 ♘g5 16 e5 ♕xf3* or *14 ... g5!? 15 ♗g3 h5 16 h3 g4* with an attack.

C

4 ♘c3

Although not particular-ly popular, this might be

White's best.

4 ... fe!?

It might also be possible to play 4 ... ♘f6 5 de ♘xe4 6 ♘xe4 fe 7 ♘g5 d5 8 e6 ♗c5 (or 8 ... ♗b4+ 9 c3 and then 9 ... ♗c5) 9 ♘xe4 ♗e7 10 ♕h5+ (10 ♘g5 ♗xg5 11 ♕h5+ g6 12 ♕xg5 ♕xg5 13 ♗xg5±) 10 ... g6 11 ♕e5 ♖f8 12 ♘g5 ♗f6 13 ♕g3 ♕e7 14 ♗e2 h6 15 ♘f3 ♕g7 but I'm not all that sure about this.

What is certain is that 4 ... **ed** is not good here: 5 ♕xd4 fe (5 ... ♘c6 can be answered by 6 ♗b5 here, in B this would have lost a tempo as the bishop had already been developed) 6 ♗g5 ♘f6 7 ♘xe4 ♗e7 8 0-0-0 (or 8 ♗c4 ♘c6 9 ♕e3±) 8 ... 0-0 9 ♘xf6+ ♗xf6 10 ♗c4+ ♔h8 11 ♗xf6 ♕xf6 12 ♕xf6 gf 13 ♘d4 ♗d7 14 ♖he1 ♘c6 15 ♘xc6 ♗xc6 16 ♖e7 ♗xg2 (Black's position was pretty miserable in any case but this simplifies White's task) 17 ♖g1 d5 18 ♗d3 ♗e4 19 ♗xe4 fe 20 ♖gg7 *(22)*

(Seventh rank absolute!) 20 ... ♖fe8 21 ♖xh7+ ♔g8 22 ♖eg7+ ♔f8 23 ♖xc7 1-0 Tseshkovsky - Inkiov. 5 ♘xd4 has also been played: 5 ... fe 6 ♕e2 d5?? (6 .. ♘f6 is fine, 7 ♘xe4 ♘xe4 8 ♕xe4+ ♕e7 or 7 ♗g5 ♗e7 8 ♘xe4 0-0) 7 ♕h5+ g6 8 ♕e5+ (oops!) 8 ... ♕e7 9

♕xh8 ♘f6 10 ♗g5 ♕b4 11 ♕xf6 ♘d7 12 ♕e6+ ♗e7 13 ♘b5 ♘f6 14 ♘xc7+ and Black resigned a few moves later, Alberts - Soria, Corr 1977. I feel that somewhere along the line, Black could have saved himself a few stamps!

5 ♘xe4 d5
6 ♘xe5?!

Theory, but not best, in my opinion. 6 ♘g3 e4 (maybe 6 ... ed 7 ♕xd4 ♘f6 8 ♗g5 ♗e7 9 0-0-0 0-0 could be tried: 10 ♗xf6 ♗xf6 11 ♕xd5+ ♕xd5 12 ♖xd5 ♗e6 is unclear; and if 10 ♗d3 h6!?. However, White's lead in development is a bit disturbing) 7 ♘e5 ♘f6 which is Bird - Morphy, London 1858, and now Keres' suggestion 8 f3! looks good: 8 ... ef 9 ♕xf3 ♗d6 10 ♗d3 0-0 11 0-0 ♘c6!? 12 ♘xc6 bc±/= but 11 ... ♘e4 and 11 ... ♘bd7 might also be possible, and better (or worse!).

6 ... de
7 ♕h5+ g6

8 ♘xg6 hg!

For some odd reason *ECO* prefers 8 ... ♘f6?? to this. Let's see their analysis: 9 ♕e5+ ♚f7 (9 ... ♗e7 10 ♘xh8 ♘c6 11 ♗b5 ♕d5 12 ♗g5± Zukertort) 10 ♗c4+ ♚g7 11 ♗h6+ (11 ♘xh8 ♚xh8 12 ♗g5 ♗g7 13 ♗xf6 ♗xf6 14 ♕xe4 ♘c6 15 0-0-0 is not bad either - Bilguer) 11 ... ♚xh6 12 ♘xh8 ♗b4+ 13 c3 ♕xh8 14 cb with big advantage to White. The question is: why should Black want to play this?

9 ♕xh8

At the last moment I noticed that White has another important possibility here, and one that seems to have escaped everyone's attention: 9 ♕xg6+!? Now 9 ... ♚d7 10 ♕f5+ ♚e8 is a forced draw if White wants it - which is as well to know if you have to play for a win at all costs with the black pieces! And White can also play 11 ♕e5+ ♗e6! 12 ♕xh8 although I think Black's two pieces are better than the rook, e.g. 12 ... ♘c6 13 ♗b5 ♕d5! 14 c4?! ♗b4+ 15 ♚f1 ♕f5 16 d5 ♗c5 17 ♕h4 e3 with a decisive attack.

9 ... ♗e6

10 ♕e5

"And with 'correct' play White should realize his advantage" - Gipslis. But isn't Black better? He has two knights for a rook and two pawns, and a target on d4. It is also important that the rooks have no open file. So, let's look at some continuations.

10 ... ♕d5

11 ♕xd5

In principle, White should want to exchange queens, and anyway 11 ♕xc7? ♗d6 12 ♕c3 ♘c6 (menacing ... ♗b4) 13 a3 ♘xd4 is already winning for Black.

11 ... ♗xd5

12 ♗e3

12 c4? ♗f7 13 ♗e3 ♗g7 (... c5 and ... ♘c6 are threats) 14 ♖d1 ♘c6 15 ♗e2 0-0-0 (or ... ♘ge7-f5)∓ 16 d5 ♘b4 winning a pawn. To make his pieces truly operational Black needs to force some weakness and find some squares for them. For instance, if White plays d5 then ... e5 and ... c5 become useful posts for Black's knights.

12 .... ♗g7

13 c3 ♘d7

14 ♗e2 ♘h6

When Black intends ... ♘f5, ... 0-0-0 (or ... ♚f7), ... c5 or whatever seems appropriate. Remember, Black only has to win the exchange and he will be a piece up!

Seriously though, when playing with two pieces

against a rook, it is generally important to avoid exchanging the other rook.

D

	4	ef	e4
	5	Ng5	Bxf5

More sensible than 5 ... Nf6 6 f3 Qe7 7 Be2 ef? 8 Nxf3 Bxf5 9 0-0 Qd7 10 d5! Be7 11 Nd4 Bg4 12 Rxf6! with a crushing advantage, Vitolins – Arhipkin, USSR 1975.

	6	Nc3	d5!
	7	f3	

"White has the better position. It's all so simple that it's difficult to find an improvement for Black" – Gipslis (or Larsen, it's not clear which). Well, maybe. What about:

	7	...	e3!?
	8	Bxe3	h6
	9	Nh3	

I think that 9 Bd3?! just loses: 9 ... Bxd3 10 Qxd3 (10 Ne6 Qd6 11 Nxf8 Ba6∓ or 11 Nxd5 Na6 12 Nxf8 Qxd5∓) 10 ... hg 11 Qg6+ Kd7 12 Nxd5 Ne7 or 12 Qf5+ Kc6! and Black should be able to consolidate his extra piece without too many problems.

9 g4!? is an interesting alternative to the text. Black's best is 9 ... hg!, e.g. 10 gf Bd6! 11 Qd2?! Bg3+ with the following possibilities: 12 hg Rxh1 13 0-0-0 Nc6∞ or 12 Kd1?! Qh4 or 12 Bf2 Bf4 (12 ... Qe7+ is also worth consideration). 11 Qe2 is better, when 11 ... Ne7?! 12 Bxg5 Bg3+ 13 hg Rxh1 14 Nxd5 Nc6 looks very dangerous for Black but may be playable and 11 ... Kf8 12 0-0-0 c6 13 Qd2 Qc7 14 Bxg5 Rh5!? or 14 ... Rxh2 is very wild.

	9	...	Bxh3
	10	gh	Be7
	11	Bf2	

Or 11 Rg1 Bh4+ 12 Bf2 Bxf2+ 13 Kxf2 Qh4+ 14 Rg3 Ne7 15 Kg1 0-0.

	11	...	Bf6
	12	Qd2	Ne7
	13	0-0-0	Nbc6

With reasonable play for the pawn, a doubled h-pawn at that.

It is difficult to be catagorical, and there are many grey areas, but I think that Mestel's variation is completely viable.

4) Larsen's Variation - Introduction

1	e4	e5
2	♘f3	d6
3	d4	ed
4	♘xd4	g6 (23)

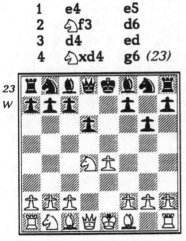

In the late '60s Danish Grandmaster Bent Larsen evolved the plan of fianchettoing his king's bishop after capturing on d4. The merits of this idea are evident: Black immediately places his king's bishop on the active a1-h8 diagonal and can bring strong pressure to bear on the squares d4 and c3. The disadvantage is that should White succeed in exchanging this bishop the dark squares around Black's king can become very vulnerable.

The positions that result are similar in many ways to those of the Sicilian Dragon (the difference being that, in the Dragon Black exerts pressure on the c-file whereas here Black presses on the e-file) or certain variations of the Pirc (from which identical positions often arise).

It is not clear that, with accurate play, White can demonstrate any real advantage. Conversely, the slightest mistake on his part can lead to immediate, catastrophic consequences.

Before proceeding with the analysis of this position I would mention that it is also possible to play the kingside fianchetto after inserting the moves 4 ... ♘f6 5 ♘c3 (and then 5 ... g6). This will most likely transpose into one of the variations considered later, but does deprive Black of some of his more interesting possibilities involving an early ... ♘c6. It does also allow White to play 6 ♗g5 although it is not clear that this is so wonderful: 6 ... ♗g7 (6 ... h6?? 7 ♗xf6 ♕xf6 8 ♘d5 ♕d8 9 ♘b5 ♘a6 10 ♕d4±) 7 ♕d2 h6 (It is best to break the pin immediately, the game Tompa – Hardicsay, Budapest 1972, continued, in entertaining fashion: 7 ... 0-0 8 0-0-0 ♖e8 9 f3 ♘c6 10 ♘xc6 - this move has its downside as well, Black can now utilize the b-file - 10 ... bc 11 h4± ♕e7 12 h5 a5 13 hg fg 14 ♗c4+ ♗e6 15 ♗xe6+ ♕xe6 16 g4 a4 17 a3 ♖ab8 18 ♖h2 ♖b7 - both sides prepare their attacks as quickly as possible, but perhaps some defensive moves should be considered - 19 ♖dh1 ♖eb8 20 ♘xa4 *(24)*

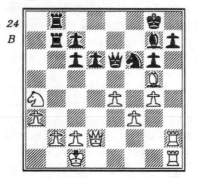

24
B

20 ... ♖xb2!? 21 ♘xb2 ♘xe4! 22 fe ♗xb2+ 23 ♔d1 ♕xg4+ 24 ♕e2 ♕xg5 25 ♕d2 ♕g4+ 26 ♕e2 ½-½ although I think that Black is now better) 8 ♗f4 g5 9 ♗g3 ♘h5 10 ♗e2 (10 ♗b5+! seems better as if either knight or bishop goes to d7, White

will play ♘f5, so: 10 ... c6 11 ♗e2 ♘xg3 12 hg ♕f6 13 ♖d1 ♕xd4 14 ♕xd4 ♗xd4 15 ♖xd4 ♔e7 16 0-0 b5 17 a4 which led to some advantage for White in the game Adorjan – Radulov, Sofia 1970, but I don't like Black's decision to give up his dark-squared bishop, 13 ... 0-0 seems better) 10 ... ♘xg3 11 hg ♘c6 12 ♗b5 ♗d7 13 ♘de2 ♕f6 14 0-0 0-0-0 when Black was fine, Hennings – Radulov, Siegen ol 1970. On the plus side, White is no longer able to play c4, so any player who is worried about this possibility might profitably be able to play this way.

Returning to the position after 4 ... g6, White can play either:

A Others
B 5 c4
C 5 ♘c3

A Other White fifth moves

Moves other than 5 c4 or 5 ♘c3 do not have any great significance, almost invariably they will transpose into variation C sooner or later, as c3 is very much the best square for the queen's knight. Some examples:

a) **5 g3** ♗g7 6 ♗g2 ♘f6 7 0-0 0-0 8 c4 ♘c6 9 ♘e2 ♗e6 10 ♘d2 ♘h5 11 h3 ♘e5 12 g4

♘f6 13 ♕c2 g5 14 ♘f3 ♘xf3+ 15 ♗xf3 ♘d7 16 ♘g3 ♘e5 17 ♗e2 ♘g6 18 ♘h5 ♗e5 19 ♖d1 ♘f4 *(25)*

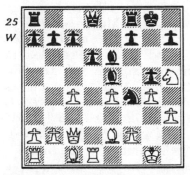

White's original opening plan has rebounded, Black's firm grip on the kingside dark squares giving him the edge, Csom - Mortenson, Biel 1978.

b) 5 ♗c4 ♗g7 6 0-0 ♘f6 and at this point, in Kavalek - Larsen, San Juan 1969, White could find nothing better than 7 ♘c3 transposing to section C3.

c) **5 h4!?** This is not such a bad idea. I'm surprised that it is not tried more often; Kaidanov - Grabusov, **USSR** 1975, continued 5 ... ♗g7 6 h5 ♘c6 7 ♗e3 ♘ge7 8 ♘c3 ♘e5 9 ♗e2±, but more sensible (to my mind at any rate) is 5... ♘f6 6 ♘c3 ♗g7 7 ♗e2 0-0 with a likely transposition to one of the later lines after 8 ♗e3, as 8 h5 ♖e8 9 hg hg 10 f3 d5 leaves the white king looking rather exposed in the middle. Two possible continuations: 11 ♗h6 de 12 ♗xg7 ♔xg7 13 fe? ♖h8! and it is Black who attacks on the h-file! Or 13 ♕d2 ♖h8 14 0-0-0 (not 14 ♖xh8? ♕xh8 15 0-0-0 ef and ... ♕h6∓) 14 ... ♘c6 15 ♘xc6 ♕xd2+ and Black is fine.

B

	5	c4		♗g7
	6		♘c3	

Larsen recalls that one of his biggest problems when preparing this line was finding a suitable answer to 5 c4. It seems almost inevitable that the game will transpose into either a line of the King's Indian Defence (variation B1) or a Modern Defence (variation B2) where White has, of course, played c4.

At the moment the line B2 is under a bit of a cloud, so I recommend line B1. I do not really want to get bogged down in a detailed examination of either line, as they can be found in books on the specific openings. It could be argued that anyone who plays 1 e4 is unlikely to be conversant with 1 d4 sidelines anyway, and this probably explains why 5 c4 is rarely played.

B1

	6	...		♘f6!

7 ♗e2

This is the most solid move, but 7 f3 is not bad; Black can effect a transposition to a rarely played line of the Samisch King's Indian: 7 ... 0-0 8 ♗e3 c6 9 ♕d2 (9 ♗e2 will return to the main line) 9 ... d5! (the key to Black's counterplay) 10 ed cd 11 0-0-0 (*11 ♗e2 ♘c6 12 c5. Obviously not 12 0-0? ♘xd4 13 ♗xd4 dc 14 ♗xc4 (26)*

26
B

14 ... ♘e4 15 fe ♕xd4+∓ Soos - Janosevic, Titovo Uzice 1966. *12 ... ♖e8 and if 13 0-0 then 13 ... ♖xe3!* is again a transfer to a position further on) 11 ... ♘c6 12 ♗h6 (Not 12 ♘xc6 bc 13 cd ♘xd5 14 ♘xd5 cd 15 ♕xd5 ♕xd5 16 ♖xd5 ♗e6∓) 12 ... ♗xh6 13 ♕xh6 ♕b6= Portisch - Gligoric, Sousse 1967. Alternatively, 10 cd cd 11 e5 ♘e8 12 f4 f6 13 ♗b5 fe 14 fe ♗xe5 15 ♘f3 ♗g7 16 0-0 ♘c6= Pachman - Gligoric, Oberhausen 1961.

7 ... 0-0

8 0-0

8 ♗e3 is also possible, 8 ... ♖e8 9 f3 (9 ♕c2 is worse: 9 ... ♕e7 10 f3 c6 11 ♗f2 ♘h5 12 g3 ♘d7-e5∓, Simagin - Petrosian, Moscow 1966) 9 ... c6! (Black's only hope for a good position resides in the possibility of forcing through ... d5 as soon as possible) 10 0-0 (*10 ♕d2 d5 11 ed cd 12 0-0. 12 c5?! ♘bd7 13 c6 ♘e5 14 cb ♗xb7 15 0-0 ♘c4∓ Simagin - Bednarski, Zinnowitz 1965. 12 0-0 was played in the eleventh game of the most recent, at the time of writing, at least!, match for the World Championship, transposing from the King's Indian, of course, Kasparov not being known for his espousal of the Philidor's, as yet! 12 ... ♘c6 13 c5 and now Kasparov uncorked the screamer of a move 13 ... ♖xe3!. Only time will tell how sound this 'shot' is, but it certainly does offer Black plenty of tactical chances on the dark squares. 14 ♕xe3 ♕f8 15 ♘xc6 bc 16 ♔h1. It was important to remove the king from the vulnerable a7-g1 diagonal. 16 ... ♖b8 17 ♘a4 ♖b4 18 b3 ♗e6 19 ♘b2 ♘h5. In order to avoid the following draw, I tried 19 ... ♖h4?! in a recent blitz game, which continued: 20 ♕f2 g5 21 g3 ♖h6 22 ♘d3*

♕b8 23 f4 ♘e4 24 ♕e3 ♗h3 25 fg ♗d4 26 ♕f4 ♕xf4 27 ♘xf4 ♗xf1 28 ♖xf1 ♘xg3+ 29 ♔g2 ♘xf1 30 gh ♘e3+ with a winning endgame, but the play is far from perfect! *20 ♘d3 ♖h4 21 ♕f2 ♕e7 22 g4 (27)*

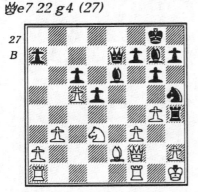

22 ♖ac1 ♗d4 was too risky for White, but now Black decides to force a perpetual check. *22 ... ♗d4! 23 ♕xd4 ♖xh2+ 24 ♔xh2 ♕h4+ ½-½* Karpov - Kasparov, New York 1990. Also *10 ♘f2 d5 11 ed cd 12 0-0 ♘c6 13 c5 ♘h5* was level in Taimanov - Stein, USSR Ch 1965) 10 ... d5 11 cd ♘xd5! 12 ♘xd5 cd 13 ♕b3 ♘c6 14 ♖ad1 ♗xd4 15 ♗xd4 ♘xd4 16 ♖xd4 ♕f6 17 ♕xd5? (17 ♕a4 ♗e6 18 ♖fd1 de 19 fe ½-½ Soltan - Danstrup, Corr 1987 was better) 17 ... ♗e6 18 ♕c5 ♖ec8 19 ♕b4 a5 20 ♕a4 ♖c2!! *(28)*
21 ♕xc2 ♕xd4+ 22 ♖f2 ♖c8 23 ♕d1 ♕xb2 24 ♗f1 ♕c1!∓ Klinger - Dorfman, Belgrade 1988.

8 ... ♖e8

9 f3

The only move to defend the pawn, 9 ♕c2? ♘xe4! 10 ♘xe4 ♗xd4 11 ♗g5 f6 12 ♖ad1 fg 13 ♖xd4 ♗f5 14 c5 ♘c6 15 ♗c4+ ♔g7 17 ♕c3 ♘xd4 17 ♕xd4+ ♔h6-+ is hopeless for White, Rosetto - Larsen, Amsterdam IZ 1964.

9 ... c6

10 ♔h1

This move will be necessary, sooner or later, to avoid tactics involving ... ♕b6+ (xb2). 10 ♘c2 ♘a6 11 ♔h1 will reach the main line position, and 11 ♗f4 d5 12 ed cd 13 cd ♘h5 14 ♗d2 ♘c7 is unclear. 10 ♗e3 is considered previously, but 10 ♗f4? attempting to pressurize d6, backfires horribly: 10 ... ♘h5! 11 ♗e3 f5 12 ♕d2 f4 13 ♗f2 ♗e5 (Black has artificially created a strong point on e5, and White is already in a bad way) 14 ♖ad1 ♕f6 15 ♘b3 ♘g3! *(29)* 16 hg fg 17 ♗e3?! ♕h4 18 ♖fe1 ♗f4! 0-1 for 19 ♗xf4

29
W

♕h2+ 20 ♔f1 ♕h1 is mate, and other tries lose a great deal of material, Porath – Gligoric, Netanya 1965.

10 ... ♘a6!

The knight is coming to c7 to lend support to the d5 break. Once this is successfully accomplished, Black will have free play for all his pieces.

11 ♘c2 ♘c7
12 ♗e3

12 ♗f4 is still of doubtful value, 12 ... d5! 13 cd cd 14 ♗xc7 ♕xc7 15 ed ♕f4!, Huzman – Epishin, USSR 1987. I like this last move which emphasizes Black's control over the central dark squares. In my opinion, Black has ample compensation for the pawn. One illustrative line: 16 ♘d4? ♘h5! 17 ♘db5 (there are no dark squares in the middle on which the white knights can feel safe) 17 ... ♗e5 18 g3 ♘xg3+ 19 hg ♕xg3 20 f4 ♗h3 21 ♗f3 ♗xf4∓).

12 ... d5

13 ed cd
14 c5 ♘h5
15 ♕d2

If instead 15 g4?! then 15 ... ♖xe3 16 ♘xe3 ♘f4 is conceivable e.g: 17 ♘g2 ♘xg2 18 ♔xg2 d4 and ♘d5∞.

15 ... d4! *(30)*

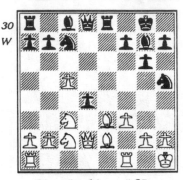

30
W

16 ♗xd4 ♗f5
17 ♘e4

Clearly forced.

17 ... ♘e6
18 ♖ad1

It may have been better to play the other rook here.

18 ... ♘xd4
19 ♘xd4 ♕h4!?

The variation 19 ... ♗xe4 20 fe ♖xe4 21 ♘f3 is assessed as ± in Informator 49, but after 21 ... ♕xd2 22 ♖xd2 ♘f4 23 ♗d1 ♘e6 I think that ∓ is more accurate!

20 ♕e1 ♕f4!?

20 ... ♕xe1 21 ♖fxe1 ♗xe4 22 fe ♖xe4 is equal.

21 g3 ♕e3

With a level position, L Hansen – Epishin, Warsaw 1990. It is evident that

Black could have reached a balanced endgame at several moments, but felt that his position justified a more ambitious approach.

Looking through these games makes me wonder why this line is not more popular with King's Indian players. It appears that White is unable to prevent Black liquidating the centre after which the black bishop tucked away on g7 exerts a powerful influence on the centre, whereas the two white bishops seem a little exposed, naked even, when the e- and d-files are opened.

B2

6 ... ♘c6!?

This is better than 6 ... ♘e7?! because 7 ♗g5 is annoying; obviously 7 ... f6 8 ♗e3 is not the kingside pawn formation that Black desires.

7 ♗e3

It doesn't make a lot of sense to take on c6: 7 ♘xc6?! bc 8 c5 ♘e7 9 cd cd 10 ♗f4 ♕a5! is an analysis of Larsen's and is clearly good for Black.

7 ... ♘ge7

It is also possible to play 7 ... ♘f6 here, but I'm not so keen on this. Rigo - Lehmann, Leipzig 1977, continued: 8 f3 0-0 9 ♗e2 ♗d7 10 0-0 a6 11 ♕d2 ♖e8 12 ♖ac1 ♕b8±.

8 h4!?

Kasparov blew the English Grandmaster Speelman away at Barcelona 1989 with this thrust, so I have taken it as my main line. The main alternative, **8 ♗e2**, is solid and good; 8 ... 0-0 9 0-0 (*9 g4 ♗e6! Despite the fine position Seirawan had in this position in his game against Naumkin, Moscow 1990, he decided to essay 9 ... f5!? 10 gf gf 11 ef ♘xd4! 12 ♗xd4 ♘xf5 13 ♗xg7 ♘xg7 instead, when he was again well placed although his king was a little exposed. 10 ♖g1 ♘xd4 11 ♗xd4 ♘c6 12 ♗xg7 ♔xg7 13 ♕d2 ♕h4∓, D Gurevich - Seirawan, USA Ch 1987. If, instead, 9 ♕d2 f5 10 ef ♗xd4 11 ♗xd4 ♘f5 12 ♗e3 ♘xe3 13 ♕xe3 ½-½ Dlugy - Seirawan, USA Ch 1987, but 9 h4 is altogether more dangerous, when the game Vilela - Popchev, Albena 1989, led to a big advantage for White after 9 ... ♘xd4 10 ♗xd4 ♗xd4 11 ♕xd4 ♗c6 12 0-0-0 ♘c6 13 ♕e3 f5 14 ef ♗xf5 15 g4!,* but 9 ... f5 would have been more of a test of White's aggression) 9 ... f5 (this is Black's only attempt to get serious counterplay and, indeed, White must be

careful) 10 ♘xc6 (the obvious *10 ef?* allows *10 ...
♗xd4! 11 ♗xd4 ♘xf5 12 ♗e3
♘xe3 13 fe∓ (31)*

31
B

Indeed, this is such a well
disguised trap that even
very strong Grandmasters
have been known to fall
into it! Two recent examples: *13 ... ♖xf1+?! 14
♕xf1 ♗e6 15 ♕f4 ♕e7 16 ♖f1
♖e8 17 ♗g4 ♘d8 18 ♗xe6+
♘xe6=* Tal - Azmaiparashvili, Albena 1984, and *16 ...
a6 17 ♗g4 ♗f7 18 ♗f3 ♖f8.
18 ... g5 is best. 19 ♘d5
♗xd5 20 ♗xd5+ ♔g7 21
♕xf8+ ♕xf8 22 ♖xf8 ♔xf8
23 ♗xc6 bc 24 b4!±* Polugaevsky - Ermenkov, Majorca 1989. Strangely, White
won both games! Of course,
the relative strengths of
the players at the time -
about 100 points more for
the Whites - may have had
something to do with it!
Anyway, 13 ... ♗e6! is better,
and conserves Black's plus.
10 ♕d2 is a sound alternative, although *10 ... fe 11*

♘xe4 ♘f5 12 ♘xf5 ♗xf5 13
♘c3 ♕f6 14 ♖fd1 ♔h8
should be equal) 10 ... bc 11
♗f3! ♖b8 12 ♕d2 c5 13 ♗g5
♕d7, Lputian - Azmaiparashvili, Erevan 1989, and
now 14 e5 would have been
strong.

Apart from 8 ♗e2, **8
♘xc6!?** has also been
played by Polugaevsky, presumably in an attempt to
improve the opening he had
against Ermenkov. Azmaiparashvili was, again, the
player of the black pieces
at Reykjavik 1990, and the
game progressed: 8 ... bc 9
♗d4 0-0 (Black played differently against Knaak, Berlin 1989: *9 ... ♗xd4 10 ♕xd4
0-0 11 c5 dc 12 ♕xc5 ♕d6 13
♕xd6 cd* but the only
change is the position of
the king on g7 and the
pawn on f6. The best move
here, though, is *9 ... f6! 10
c5! d5 11 ♗e2 0-0 12 0-0* and,
according to Seirawan, 12 ...
♗e6 would have been equal
in his game against Alburt,
US Ch 1990) 10 ♗xg7 ♔xg7
11 ♕d4+ f6 12 c5 dc 13 ♕xc5
♕d6 14 ♕xd6 with a slight
edge for White. However, 8
... ♘xc6 is more natural,
and following 9 ♗e2 0-0 10
0-0 f5 11 ef ♗xf5, say, Black
has an active position. 9 c5
can be simply answered by
9 ... dc 10 ♕xd8 ♘xd8 11
♗xc5 ♘e6= and 9 ♕d2 ♗e6

10 ♗e2 ♛d7 11 0-0 0-0 was fine for Black in Yakovich - Kantslar, Uzhgorod 1987; ... f5 is coming.

8 ... h6?!

Kasparov considers this dubious, and certainly it does seem that if Black wishes to play f5, then ... h6 first further weakens his kingside. On the other hand, the immediate ... f5 also has its drawbacks: 8 ... f5!? 9 h5 fe 10 hg (this appears to be stronger than 10 ♘xe4 ♘f5 11 ♗g5 ♛d7 12 ♘f6+ ♗xf6 13 ♗xf6 0-0 14 ♘xf5 ♛xf5 15 ♗d4 ♛e4+ 16 ♗e3 ♘b4 17 ♖c1 ♗f5 which is very wild, Vaganian - Mestel, Hastings 1974/5) 10 ... ♘xg6 11 ♛d2 ♘xd4 12 ♗xd4 ♘e5 13 ♘xe4 ♛e7 14 0-0-0± , when the black king position looks very windy, Bonsch - Azmaiparashvili, Dortmund 1990.

9 ♗e2

9 ♛d2 also has its points: 9 ... ♘e5 10 0-0-0 a6 (10 ... ♘7c6 can't be worse, but after 11 f3 ♗e6 12 ♘xe6 fe 13 ♗e2 ♛e7 14 f4 ♘f7 15 ♗f3 a6 16 ♛c2 White had a clear plus in Westerinen - Wahlbom, Gausdal 1978) 11 ♗e2 ♗d7 12 ♔b1 h5 13 f3 c6 14 ♘b3 ♗e6 15 ♛xd6 ♛xd6 16 ♖xd6 ♗xc4 17 ♘a5!± Podgaets - Azmaiparashvili, Haifa 1989.

9 ... f5

10 ef ♘xf5
11 ♘xf5 ♗xf5
12 ♛d2 ♛d7?

12 ... ♛f6!? was a better choice.

13 0-0! 0-0-0?!

Black castles queenside, where his king will have more pawn cover, but it is not enough to save him.

14 b4! (32)

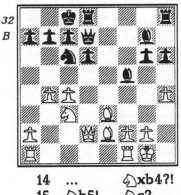

14 ... ♘xb4?!
15 ♘b5! ♘c2
16 ♗f3! d5
17 ♗xd5 ♘xa1

Black finally decides to take the rook, which has been on offer for several moves, but in return he will have to give up his queen to avoid mate.

18 ♘xa7+ ♔b8
19 ♛b4 ♛xd5

19 ... c5 20 ♗f4+! ♔a8 21 ♛a5 is curtains.

20 cd ♘c2

And the game finished: 21 ♛a5 ♘xe3 22 fe ♖he8 23 ♘b5 ♖xd5 24 ♛xc7+ ♔a8 25 ♛a5+ 1-0.

These two variations

seem to fairly reflect the state of the two openings at present: whereas the King's Indian has a good reputation, and even holds its own at World Championship level (when played by Kasparov, at least!), the Modern still has a doubtful look about it. Even great connoisseurs of the Modern Defence like Azmaiparashvili seem to lose an awful lot of games with Black.

C

5   ♘c3   ♗g7 *(33)*

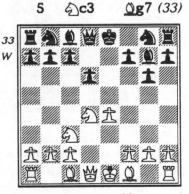

This is, in effect, the starting position for Larsen's variation, as 5 ♘c3 is by far the most popular choice.

Now there are the following possibilities:

C1 6 g3
C2 6 ♗e2
C3 6 ♗c4
C4 6 ♗f4

The best move, 6 ♗e3, is considered in the next chapter.

Whilst writing this section, it occurred to me that 6 ♗d3!? is not as ridiculous as it looks, for 6 ... ♗xd4 7 ♗b5+ c6 8 ♕xd4 is clearly better for White. 6 ... ♘c6 7 ♘xc6 bc 8 0-0 ♖b8 might be Black's best, his centre is strong and the pressure on the b-file augments that along the a1-h8 diagonal.

C1

6   g3   ♘c6
7   ♗e3   ♘f6
8   h3   0-0
9   ♗g2   ♖e8

Black has been successful with 9 ... ♘e5 in practice: 10 0-0 a6 (10 ... ♖e8 11 b3 c6 12 ♖e1 ♕c7 13 a4 ♘ed7 14 ♕d2 ♘c5 15 ♗h6 a5 16 g4 ♗h8 17 ♖ad1 ♗d7 18 ♗f4 ♖ad8 and instead of 19 g5?. Rojas - Dreev, Paris 1984. when White was struggling, 19 ♗g3 was equal) 11 a4 ♖b8 12 ♖e1 ♖e8 13 f4? (13 b3 first) 13 ... ♘c4 14 ♗c1 c5! 15 ♘b3 ♗e6 16 ♔h2 b5 17 ab ab 18 e5 b4! *(34)*
19 ♘d5 (19 ef bc 20 fg cb will win a pawn) 19 ... ♘xd5 20 ♗xd5 ♗xd5 21 ♕xd5 ♘b6 22 ♕f3 de∓ Oim - Tal, Viljandi 1972. However, despite this, I think the text is better.

10   0-0   ♗d7

10 ... ♘xd4 worked out quite well in the game Byrne – Larsen, Lugano 1979: 11 ♗xd4 ♗d7 12 ♕d3 ♗c6 13 ♖fe1 when according to Larsen, either ... ♘d7 or ... a5 were equal, instead: 13 ... ♖e7? 14 ♖e3 ♕f8 15 ♖ae1 ♘d7 16 ♗xg7 ♕xg7 17 b4 was better for White. Black should be fine provided he can restrain the white e-pawn in the style of Nimzowitsch.

The position after 10 ... ♗d7 is one I've had myself, but from a Pirc defence; I feel that Black's resources are suffcient.

    11 ♖e1   a6
    12 a4

Instead 12 f4 ♘xd4 13 ♗xd4 c5 14 ♗xf6!? ♗xf6 15 ♕xd6 ♗d4+ 16 ♔h2 ♖e6 17 ♕d5 ♖b6 gives Black great play for the pawn, Byrne – Christiansen, USA Ch 1984.

    12 ...   ♘b4

The weakened b4 is a tempting site for a knight, but 12 ... ♘a5!? is also interesting: 13 g4 c5 14 ♘de2 ♗c6 15 ♘g3 ♕b6 16 ♖b1 ♘c4 17 ♗f4 ♕a5 18 ♕d3 ♕b4 19 ♘a2 ♕xa4 20 ♘c3 ♕b4 21 ♘a2 ♕b5 22 ♘c3 ♘xb2∓ Wockenfuss – Plaskett, Lugano 1986.

    13 ♕d2   c5
    14 ♘b3   ♗c6 *(35)*

The idea of taking on d4 and then playing c5 is a very common one in the Philidor. Here it solves all Black's problems. 15 ♗f4 would now have been level. as it was, Sek – Ksieski, Poland 1981, continued 15 f3 ♕c7 16 ♘e2 ♖ad8 17 c3 d5 18 ♗f4 ♕b6 19 e5 ♘e4! with a powerful initiative.

C2

    6 ♗e2

This is rather insipid.

    6 ...   ♘c6
    7 ♗e3   ♘f6
    8 0-0   0-0
    9 ♖e1

If instead 9 ♕d2 ♖e8 10 ♘xc6 bc 11 ♗f3 ♗b7 we reach the identical position to one that arose in Spassky - Larsen, Malmo 1968, from a Three Knights game. (Incidentally, a word of advice for anyone planning to write a book about a particular opening; avoid those openings that can arise from a number of different move orders, as you will spend all your time wondering whether the pieces really are on the right squares!) Back to the game: 12 ♗h6? (12 ♖fe1 was correct) 12 ... ♗xh6 13 ♕xh6 ♖e5! 14 ♖ae1 c5 15 ♖e3 ♕e7 16 ♖fe1 ♖ae8. This deserves a diagram (36). Almost all the pieces on the board are either defending or attacking (restraining) the e-pawn. I am sure that Nimzowitsch would have enjoyed this game very much.

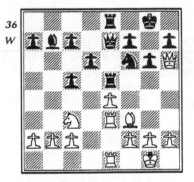

36
W

17 h4 ♕e6 18 ♕f4 (White fails to find the best chance, 18 b3!) 18 ... ♔g7 19 b3 h6 20 ♕g3 ♕d7 21 ♕f4

♖8e7 22 ♘d5? (22 ♖3e2 g5 23 hg hg 24 ♕g3 g4 25 ♖e3 ♔f8 26 ♗d1 was only a little plus for Black) 22 ... ♗xd5 23 ed g5! 24 hg hg 25 ♕g3 ♕f5 26 c4 ♖xe3 27 fe ♖e5 28 ♗d1 ♕d3 29 ♗f3 ♕c3 30 ♔h2 a5 (Black has posted all his pieces on black squares which guarantees that the light-squared bishop will not be a problem) 31 ♔h1 ♔f8 32 ♖f1 ♕xe3 33 ♕h3 ♔g7 34 g3 ♕d4 35 g4 a4 36 ♗d1 ♖e3 37 ♕g2 ♖d3 38 ♗e2 ♖d2 39 ba ♕e5 0-1.

| 9 | ... | ♖e8 |
| 10 | ♘xc6 | bc |

I think that this exchange tends to favour Black more than White, the b-file and extra control over the centre can be very useful.

11	♗f3	♘d7
12	♕d2	♗a6
13	♖ad1	♕b8

Black has a very pleasant position.

| 14 | b3 | ♕b4 |
| 15 | ♘b1 | ♕xd2 |

And after some ups and downs Black achieved a draw, Karpov - Keene, Bad Lautenberg 1977. To score ½ out of 2 Whites is not an impressive result from two such strong players as Spassky and Karpov. Therefore we can surmise that 6 ♗e2 is not particularly troublesome.

C3

6 ♗c4

A logical and aggressive move, but the bishop may find itself more than a little exposed here.

6 ... ♘c6!

It is also possible to play 6 ... ♘f6 but I don't think that this puts White's move to the test: 7 0-0 0-0 8 ♗g5 h6 9 ♗h4 ♘c6 (9 ... a6?! seems a trifle slow, and in the game Brustman - Landry, Dubai ol 1986, Black's subsequent play did not exactly help matters: 10 f4 ♕e8 11 ♗xf6 ♗xf6 12 ♘d5 ♗d8 13 f5 g5 14 ♕h5 c5 15 ♕xh6 ♕xe4 16 f6 ♕g6 17 ♘e7+ ♗xe7 and 1-0 before White could play 18 ♕xg6+) 10 ♘xc6 bc 11 ♕f3? (a mistake that allows Black to take the initiative, 11 f4 keeps up the pressure, when after 11 ... ♕e8 Larsen assesses the position as unclear) 11 ... g5! 12 ♗g3 ♘g4 13 ♖ad1 ♘e5 14 ♕e2 a5 15 ♗xe5 ♗xe5 16 ♖d3 ♔g7 17 g3, Kavalek - Larsen, San Juan 1969, and now 17 ... g4 was ∓.

7 ♗e3

As usual, 7 ♘xc6 only helps Black by strengthening his centre and opening up the b-file: 7 ... bc 8 0-0 (8 ♗f4? will transpose to Hazai - Sax in C4) 8 ... ♖b8! (this move very much appeals to me, but many other moves are possible; Larsen himself played 8 ... ♘e7, against Browne, San Juan 1969, and in his annotations suggests 8 ... ♗e6!? - but not 8 ... ♘f6? 9 e5! de 10 ♕xd8+ ♔xd8 11 ♗xf7. After 8 ... ♘e7 the game proceeded *9 f4 ♗e6 10 ♗d3 ♕d7 11 ♕f3 f5 12 ♗d2 0-0 13 ♖ae1 ♖ae8=*) 9 f4 (according to Harding, 9 ♗b3 ♕h4!? 10 ♕f3 ♘f6 11 e5 de 12 ♕xc6+ ♗d7 13 ♕xc7 0-0 will give Black enough compensation for the pawns - after 14 ♕xe5 - that he has sacrificed, but this is not so. The white position is solid, and he is not really behind in development; 9 ... ♗e6 or 9 ... ♘e7 are better) 9 ... ♕h4! 10 ♕d3 ♘h6! (highly original development, the knight threatens to come to g4 whilst keeping the dark squared bishop's diagonal open) 11 h3 0-0 12 b3? (White doesn't realize the danger he is in, now Black forces the win with some neat tactics) 12 ... d5! *(37)* 13 ed cd 14 ♗xd5 ♗f5 15 ♕f3 c6! 16 ♗xc6 ♗g4! 17 hg ♗d4+ 18 ♗e3 ♘xg4 19 ♕xg4 ♗xe3+ 0-1 Sherman - J Littlewood, London 1973.

7 ... ♘f6

A game of mine, from the Antibes semi-rapid tournament 1991, took a

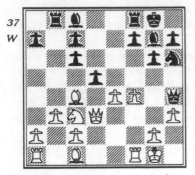

37
W

different course: 7 ... ♘ge7 8 0-0 ♘e5! 9 ♗b3 0-0 (now White has two threats to worry about, ... ♘g4 and ... c5 - c4) 10 ♗g5 h6 11 ♗h4 g5! 12 ♗g3 ♘7g6 (by controlling f4 Black secures the future of the knight on e5) 13 ♘f5 ♗xf5 14 ef ♘f4 15 ♗xf4 gf 16 ♕h5 c6 (playing ... c6 and ... d5, Black can use his extra centre pawn to shut out the white bishop) 17 ♖ad1 d5 18 ♘e4 ♘d7! 19 ♘c3 ♕g5 20 ♕xg5 hg 21 ♖fe1 ♖fe8 22 ♔f1 ♗xc3!? 23 bc ♘b6 24 h4 gh 25 ♖d4 ♖xe1+ 26 ♔xe1 c5 27 ♖xf4 c4 winning.

8 f3   0-0
9 ♕d2

White should make haste to castle queenside, as evidenced by the game Karoly - Tompa, Hungary 1978: 9 a3?! (played presumably in order to preserve his king's bishop on the a2-g8 diagonal should Black play ... ♘e5 or ... ♘a5) 9 ... ♖e8 10 ♕d2 d5! 11 ♘xc6 (11 ♘xd5?

♘xd5 12 ♗xd5? ♘xd4 13 ♗xd4 ♕xd5 wins a whole piece) 11 ... bc 12 ed (12 ♘e2 is an improvement, but 12 ... de 13 ♕xd8 ♖xd8 14 fe ♖b8 is still clearly better for Black) 12 ... ♗h6 13 ♘d1 cd 14 ♗b5 ♖xe3+! 15 ♘xe3 d4 16 ♖d1 ♕e7 17 ♕xd4 ♗xe3 (winning, of course, but missing the prettier tactics 17 ... ♗d7! 18 ♗xd7 ♗xe3 19 ♕d3 ♘xd7 20 ♕xd7 ♗d2++! (38)

38
W

Cutting off the white queen from her defender, 20 ♕e4 ♖e8 is also winning) 18 ♕d8+ ♕xd8 19 ♖xd8+ ♔g7 20 ♗a6 ♗b7 21 ♖xa8 ♗xa8 22 ♔e2 ♗d4∓.

9 ...   a6
10 0-0-0 ♘e5!

The position is similar to those of the next chapter but with the difference that White king's bishop is on c4. This allows Black to gain a vital tempo. 10 ... ♖e8 is also a good move, but 10 ... ♘xd4 is a mistake. Hoiberg - Soerenson, Phja

1986, continuing: 11 ♗xd4 b5 12 ♗d5 ♞xd5 13 ♗xg7 ♔xg7 14 ♞xd5 f6?! 15 g4 ♗e6 16 ♞f4 ♗f7 17 h4 when Black was in big trouble.

11 ♗e2

The bishop must leave the a2-g8 diagonal, as 11 ♗b3? (11 ♗d5? c6 12 ♗b3 c5 alters nothing - except the number of moves played!) 11 ... c5! 12 ♞de2 c4 13 f4 (13 ♗a4 b5 incarcerates the bishop) 13 ... cb 14 fe ♞xe4! 15 ♞xe4? ba *(39)* is easily winning for Black, no power on earth with be able to stop the a-pawn from becoming a queen.

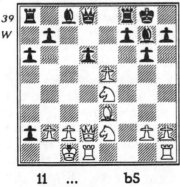

39
W

11 ... b5
12 h4

Black will treat 12 g4 in the same manner; but the attempt to avoid what follows, 12 ♞d5 loses in an unusual way: 12 ... c5! 13 ♞xf6+ (13 ♞b3 immediately makes little difference: 13 ... ♞c4! 14 ♗xc4 bc 15 ♞a5? ♞xd5 16 ♕xd5 ♕xa5 17 ♕xa8 ♕xa2 - 17 ... c3 may win even more

quickly - 18 c3 ♕d7 19 ♕d5 ♕a1+ with a devastating attack) 13 ... ♗xf6 14 ♞b3 ♞c4! 15 ♗xc4 bc 16 ♞a5 *(40)* (16 ♞a1 c3 17 bc ♕a5∓)

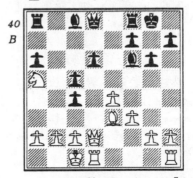

40
B

16 ... c3?! 17 ♕xd6 cb+ 18 ♔b1 ♕xa5 19 ♕xf6 ♗e6 20 ♖d5 ♗xd5 21 ed ♕d8! guarding the kingside dark squares. when Black should be able to make his material advantage count without too many problems, but 16 ... ♗e6! is probably even more effective as it is not possible to stop ... c3 or ... ♕b6 on the next move, when White can happily resign.

12	...	c5!
13	♞b3	c4!
14	♞d4	b4
15	♞d5	♞xd5
16	ed	♕a5 *(41)*

According to my analysis, Black has a decisive attack, e.g: 17 ♗h6 c3 or 17 c3 ♕xa2 18 cb ♗d7, menacing ... ♗a4 and ... ♕a1 mate. The lines demonstrate the catastrophes awaiting any unsuspecting

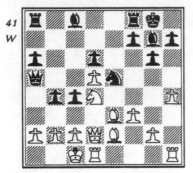

41
W

white player should he commit the very slightest slip-up against Philidor's Defence.

C4
6 ♗f4

This has the same aggressive intentions as 6 ♗e3 (which is the subject of the next chapter). However, 6 ♗f4 suffers the handicap that it fails to defend d4, without any compensating advantages.

6 ... ♘c6!

Again, this is the most pertinent reply. 6 ... ♘f6 is possible: 7 ♕d2 0-0 (7 ... ♘c6 8 ♘xc6 bc 9 0-0-0 ♗e6 10 ♗h6 0-0 11 ♗xg7 ♔xg7 12 h4 h5 13 f3 ♖b8 14 ♗e2± Jansa - Castro, Malta 1980) 8 0-0-0 ♖e8 9 f3 ♘c6 10 ♘xc6 (but not 10 ♗h6? ♘xe4!) 10 ... bc 11 e5!? (This is the idea behind 6 ♗f4, but it's not particularly terrifying, 11 ♗c4 ♗e6? - 11 ♖b8 is better, in Harding's opinion - 12 ♗xe6 ♖xe6 13 e5

♘d5 - 13 ... ♘e8 looks sounder - 14 ♘xd5 cd 15 ed ♖b8 16 c3 cd 17 ♕xd5 ♕c8 18 ♖d3 ♖e2 19 ♕xd6!± Bykhovsky - Pripis, USSR 1973) 11 ... ♘d5 12 ♘xd5 cd 13 ♗g5! (this is stronger than 13 ♕xd5 ♖b8 14 c3 ♗xe5! with the attack, not 14 ... ♕d7? 15 ed ♗b7 16 ♕a5 cd 17 ♗c4 ♖bc8 18 ♖xd6± Zatulowskaja - Kushnir, Match 1971) 13 .. ♕d7 14 ♕xd5 ♖b8 15 ♗f6 ♗xf6 16 ef and now, instead of 16 ... ♕e6 17 ♕xe6 ♖xe6 18 ♖d5±, Tal - Larsen, 2nd Match game 1969, Larsen says that it was a shame that he did not play 16 ... ♕a4 17 ♗c4!? ♗e6 18 ♕d2, threatening ♕h6, 18 ... ♖xb2! with interesting complications.

7 ♘xc6

Virtually forced, 7 ♗e3 would be a most ignominious retreat, and 7 ♗b5 ♘e7 8 0-0 0-0 9 ♘xc6 ♘xc6 is very pleasant for Black indeed; a variation of the Ruy Lopez where Black has managed to dispense with ... ♗d7.

7 ... bc
8 ♗c4

This is a mish-mash of two not very good systems, 6 ♗f4 and 6 ♗c4. 8 ♕d2 seems a better bet, but I think that Black can make good use of the open b-file, e.g: 8 ... ♖b8 9 0-0-0

♗e6 10 ♘d3 ♕c8!? intending to play ... ♕b7 and commence queenside operations before castling.

8	...	♖b8
9	♕c1?!	

Obviously 9 ♗b3 would be better, with a level position.

9	...	d5!
10	ed	♖b4
11	♗b3	♕e7+ *(42)*

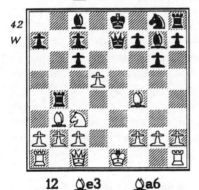

12	♗e3	♗a6

Catching the white king in the centre.

13 ♕d2?

A wasted move in a desperate situation. Black now forces the win with a series of beautiful blows.

13	...	♖d4
14	♕c1	♘f6
15	f3	♗h6
16	♔f2	♘g4+!
17	fg	♕f6+
18	♔g1?	

It would have been better to have played 18 ♔e1 ♕e5 19 ♘d1 ♗xe3 20 ♘xe3, although here too Black is winning easily after 20 ... ♖e4.

18	...	♖d1+!! *(43)*
	0-1	

Hazai – Sax, Budapest 1971, as both 19 ♕xd1 ♗xe3 and 19 ♘xd1 ♕f1 are checkmate. Very visual!!

5) Larsen's Variation - Pseudo-Yugoslav Attack

1	e4	e5
2	♘f3	d6
3	d4	ed
4	♘xd4	g6
5	♘c3	♗g7
6	♗e3!	(44)

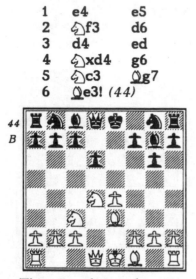

This is the only move, other than possibly 5 c4 (see previous chapter), to cause Black any anguish. White will play ♕d2, 0-0-0 and then push his h- and g-pawns whilst at the same time attempting to swap-off Black's bishop on g7. This is, to all intents and purposes, the same plan employed in the Yugoslav attack against the Sicilian Dragon. The difference is that in the Philidor's Black has use of an open e-file instead of an open c-file, as in the Dragon.

In both lines the play is sharp and uncompromising, but a peculiarity of Larsen's variation is that, at any moment, Black's queen-side pawns can advance 'a tempo', pushing White's minor pieces from the centre and then breaking open the white king's position.

6	...	♘f6

6 ... ♘c6 loses much of its point here as the d4 square is well guarded.

7	♕d2

The principal move, and by far the best. Other moves are possible but, bearing in mind that Black is threatening the annoying ... ♘g4, the only sensible moves are 7 f3 and 7 ♗e2. The former will transpose to a line considered later whilst for the latter transposition to 6 ♗e2 of the previous chapter is likely. The only independent example of this particular move order that I know of

is a game of mine: Carrasco
- Kosten, Aubervilliers Rapid Handicap 1991 (the 'Handicap' is not to signify that
the author suffers from
any serious physical problem, but rather that I had
to move considerably fas-
ter than my opponent. Certain tournament organisers
seem to be of the opinion
that chess players should
be penalized if they are too
strong!): 7 ♗e2 0-0 8 f4?
(too ambitious) 8 ... ♖e8 9
♗f3 (White's position appears to be reasonable en-
ough, but the opposition of
black rook versus white
king on the e-file - which
is a recurring motif in this
system - allows Black to
wrap up the game in short
time) 9 ... ♘xe4 10 ♗xe4 (10
♘xe4 is no better, Black
will gain at least a pawn
e.g. 10 ... d5 11 ♘c3 ♖xe3+ 12
♔f2 c5! 13 ♔xe3 cd+ 14 ♔f2
dc∓ or 13 ♘de2 d4) 10 ... d5!
11 ♗xd5 ♖xe3+ 12 ♘de2
♗xc3+ 13 bc ♕h4+ (White
was hoping to play ♗xf7+,
uncovering an attack on
Black's unguarded queen)
14 g3 ♕e7 15 ♔f2 ♗g4 *(45)*
and White soon threw in
the towel.

the game has transposed to
an old line of the Ruy Lopez, Steinitz Variation; *8 ...
♗d7 9 f3.* 9 ♗xc6! bc 10 ♘h6
♗xh6?! 11 ♕xh6 ♘g4 12 ♕d2
led to a slight White ad-
vantage in Holmov - Kim-
elfeld, Moscow 1969. *9 ...
0-0 10 0-0-0.* 10 0-0, whilst
not losing a pawn is, at
best, rather insipid. Diaz -
Razuvaev, Cienfuegos 1975,
continued: 10 ... ♖e8 11 ♖fe1
a6 12 ♘xc6 ♗xc6 13 ♗xc6 bc
14 ♘a4 ♕b8 15 ♖ad1 a5 16 b3
♘d7 17 ♗f2 ♖e6! 18 ♔h1?!
♕b7 19 ♕d3?! ♖ae8 when
Black had the better prospects. *10 ... ♘xd4!* 10 ...
a6!? 11 ♗e2 b5 12 h4 ♘e5 13
♗h6 Em. Lasker - Vidmar,
St Petersburg 1909, is also
playable if, instead of 13 ...
♘c4, Black had continued
13 ... c5 14 ♘b3 c4 15 ♘d4
b4 16 ♘d5 ♘xd5 17 ed c3
with a vicious attack. *11
♗xd4 ♘xe4! 12 fe ♗xd4 13
♕xd4 ♗xb5 14 ♘d5 f5* when
Black has won a pawn due
to the check at g5, Vyed -

7 ... 0-0

The alternatives are as
follows:

a) 7 ... ♘c6 8 0-0-0 *(8
♗b5 is also possible, when*

Szabo, 1962) 8 ... ♘g4?! (I prefer 8 ... 0-0, returning to the text) 9 ♘xc6? (what did Black intend against 9 ♗g5!?. Perhaps 9 ... ♗f6; the tactic 9 ... ♕xg5 10 ♕xg5 ♗h6 11 ♕xh6 ♘xh6 12 ♘db5 ♔d8 13 f4 left Black poorly placed in the game Dvojris - Golovin, USSR 1976) 9 ... bc 10 ♗d4 ♗xd4 11 ♕xd4 ♕f6 12 f3 ♕xd4 13 ♖xd4 ♘e3 14 ♘d1 ♘xd1 15 ♔xd1 ♔e7 with a level ending in Bellon - Karpov, Las Palmas 1977; although that didn't stop Karpov from grinding out the win.

b) 7 ... d5? 8 0-0-0 de 9 ♗h6! and White won quickly, Stanciu - Radulescu, Romania 1971.

c) 7 ... a6?! 8 0-0-0 b5 9 ♗h6 0-0 10 ♗xg7 ♔xg7 11 e5! ♘e8 (11 ... de? 12 ♘f5+ or 12 ♘e6+ wins) 12 h4 h5 13 f3 ♗b7 14 g4 ♖h8 15 e6 and the black position was quickly routed, Chabanon - Radulov, Sofia 1990.

d) 7 ... ♘g4? is now answered by 8 ♗g5.

8   0-0-0

As ... ♘g4 is no longer a problem, White tucks his king away. 8 ♗e2, which could arise from various move orders, is well met by 8 ... ♖e8 9 ♗f3 ♘c6 for 9 f3?! allows 9 ... d5!.

8 f3 is an inaccuracy, 8 ... d5! being a strong reply.

Actually, a number of the games in this chapter started with this move sequence, and most Black's transposed to the main line with 8 ... ♘c6. Why they didn't avail themselves of the opportunity to play ... d5, I don't know. After 8 f3 d5 White should play 9 0-0-0! (this is only possible due to a tactical trick, if instead *9 e5!?* then either *9 ... ♘fd7 10 e6.* 10 f4? c5. 10 ... ♘e5 11 ef+ ♘xf7* or the challenging *9 ... ♘h5!?* with the possible continuations: *10 g4 c5 11 gh cd 12 ♗xd4 ♕h4+ 13 ♗f2 ♕xh5,* which leaves the white position in disarray, e.g: *14 f4 d4! 15 ♗xd4 ♘c6* menacing ... ♖d8 and ... ♗g4; or *11 ♘b3 d4 12 0-0-0 ♘c6 13 gh.* 13 ♗g5 dc! *13 ... de*; or *10 ♗g5 ♕e8* with either ... ♕xe5, ... f6 or ... c5 coming next are both possible. However, the best move, and the one that occurred to me only after I had completed the original manuscript, may well turn out to be *9 ... ♖e8!!* with the following possibilities: *10 ef.* 10 f4 c5. *10 ... ♗h6 11 ♘d1.* 11 ♘e4!? ♗xe3 12 ♕xe3 de and 13 ... ♕xf6∓. *11 ... c5 12 ♗e2.* Not 12 ♗b5 cd 13 ♗xe8 de 14 ♘xe3 ♕xe8∓ or 12 ♔f2 ♗xe3+ 13 ♘xe3 cd 14 ♕xd4 ♘c6 with a strong initiative. *12 ... ♖xe3!? 13*

♘xe3 cd 14 ♕xd4 ♘c6 15
♕d3 d4. Or 15 ... ♘b4 menacing ... ♗xe3 and ... ♘xc2+.
16 ♘g4 ♗xg4 17 fg ♕xf6
with many threats. 9 ed? is
worse: 9 ... ♘xd5 10 ♘xd5
♕xd5 and as 11 0-0-0 fails
to 11 ... ♕xa2, and 11 ♗e2
♖e8 12 0-0?? to 12 ... ♖xe3,
White is struggling) 9 ...
de! (9 ... c5? looks good,
and in fact proved too
tempting for Black in the
game Sveshnikov - Zaichik,
Volgodonsk 1983, but after
10 ♘b3 d4 11 ♗g5 Black dis-
covered that he was unable
to take the piece on c3, so
11 ... ♘c6 12 ♘d5 b6, when
he was a little worse and
lost quickly) 10 ♗h6! (This
saves White's bacon. In the
game C Hansen - Kristian-
sen, White was quickly
overrun after 10 fe ♖e8 11
♗c4 ♘bd7 12 ♘f3 ♕e7 13
♖he1 ♘b6 14 ♗b3 ♗e6 15
♘d5. White has managed to
rid himself of the isolated
e-pawn, but the black
pieces remain well-placed.
15 ... ♗xd5 16 ed ♘e4 17 ♕a5
♕d6 18 ♔b1 ♖ad8 19 ♕xa7?
Too greedy, but 19 ♗d4
♗xd4 20 ♘xd4 ♕xh2 was
also good for Black. Now
Black whips up an over-
whelming attack. 19 ... ♖a8
20 ♕xb7 ♗xb2! (46)
21 ♗xb6. 21 ♔xb2 was im-
possible: 21 ... ♕a3+ 22 ♔a1
♘c3 leaves White no de-

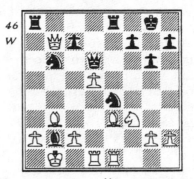

46
w

fence to 23 ... ♕xa2+ and 24
... ♖xa2 mate. 21 ... ♕a3 22
c4. Trying to give his king
some more elbow room, 22
♖xe4 ♗c3! and ... ♕b2 is
mate. 22 ... cb 23 ♔c2 ♗g7
24 ♘d4 ♘c5 25 ♖xe8+ ♖xe8
26 ♕xb6 ♖e2+ 27 ♖d2 ♖xd2+
28 ♔xd2 ♗xd4 0-1) 10 ...
♘c6 (obviously not 10 ...
♗xh6? 11 ♕xh6 ef because
of 12 ♘f5±, and similarly 10
... ef? 11 ♗xg7 ♔xg7 12 ♘f5+
and 13 ♕xd8±. However, 10
... ♘bd7 11 ♗xg7 ♔xg7 12 fe
♕e7 (or 12 ... ♖e8) or 11
♘f5? ♗xh6! 12 ♘xh6+ ♔g7
both look very pleasant for
Black. White has an iso-
lated e-pawn which leaves
the e5 square in Black's
possession but, as far as I
know, this has not been
tried as yet. The text is
more forcing) 11 ♗xg7 ♔xg7
12 ♘xc6 ♕xd2+ 13 ♖xd2 bc
14 ♘xe4 ♘xe4 15 fe and, in
Nunn's opinion, White has a
minute advantage. Perso-
nally, I'm not even sure he
has that. For instance, 15 ...

♖e8 16 ♘d3 ♗e6 17 e5!? (if
Black gets the chance he
will play ... ♔f6-e5!? when
his king will be very dominant - his queenside pawns
are more than balanced by
White's weak e-pawn and
the e5 square) 17 ... ♖ad8 18
♗e4!? ♖xd2 19 ♔xd2 ♘d5 20
♗xd5 cd 21 ♖e1=.

8 ♗h6 is quite playable,
then 8 ... ♖e8 forces 9 f3
(the intermediate move 9
♗xg7 being met by the in-
termediate move 9 ... ♘xe4!)
when 9 ... ♗h8 10 0-0-0 is
variation C.

Now, after 8 0-0-0, we
reach a parting of the ways
(47):

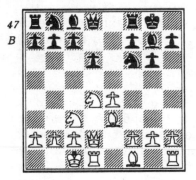

47
B

A 8 ... ♘c6
B 8 ... ♖e8

In variation A, Black in-
tends to capture on d4,
play ... ♗e6, and then sweep
up the queenside with ... c5,
... ♕a5, and then ... b5-b4.
As the white bishop will
have to retake on d4, there

is no immediate risk of
White playing ♗h6, ex-
changing Black's powerful
king's bishop, so Black
tries to avoid playing ...
♖e8.

In variation B, Black
plays ... ♖e8, so that he
will be able to drop his
bishop back to h8 should
White play ♗h6, after this
he can choose from a var-
iety of plans, the best of
these being to play ... ♘c6 -
e5, before commencing the
queenside advance.

A

8 ... ♘c6
9 f3

This is White's strongest
option, safeguarding his
centre and preparing the g4
push. There are more direct
methods available, though:

a) **9 ♘xc6** bc 10 ♗h6 (*10
e5?!* peters out fairly quickly, Keene analyses *10 ...
♘d5! 11 ♘xd5 cd 12 ed. Not
12 ♕xd5? ♗e6 and 13 ... ♗xe5
when the black bishops
point menacingly at the
white king. 12 ... ♕xd6 13
♕xd5.* 13 ♗d4 ♗xd4 14 ♕xd4
♗e6 and 15 ... c5. *13 ... ♖b8!
14 ♕xd6.* 14 c3? ♗xc3 15
♕xd6 ♗xb2+ 16 ♔c2 cd∓ as
the white king is exposed;
or 15 bc? ♕a3+-+. *14 ...
♗xb2+ 15 ♔d2 cd=*) 10 ...
♗xh6! (This is a profound
move. Black realizes that

the white queen is less active on h6 than on d2, and it will take White a long time to generate mating threats. Black, on the other hand, has an open b-file. In the game Veroci - Petronic-Ivanka, Hungary 1977, Black played without a clear plan and was soon lost: 10 ... ♖e8?! 11 ♗xg7 ♔xg7 12 ♘d3 ♗b7? - 12 ... ♗d7 13 f4 ♕b8!± - 13 f4 ♖b8 14 h3 d5 15 e5 ♘d7 16 h4 h5 17 g4±. Instead of 10 ... ♖e8?!, Heiling suggests either 10 ... ♗e6 11 ♗xg7 ♔xg7 12 f4 ♕b8 13 ♘d3 ♕b4 14 f5 ♖ab8 or 10 ... ♗d7!? 11 ♗xg7 ♔xg7 12 f4 ♕b8 13 e5 de 14 fe ♘d5 15 ♘xd5 cd 16 ♕xd5 ♗e6, both of which are unclear. At any rate, the moral is clear: Black should seek to exploit the b-file as soon as possible) 11 ♕xh6 ♖b8! (clearly this is where the rook belongs, so why not put it there immediately?) 12 f3 ♕e7 13 h4 d5! 14 h5 *(48)*

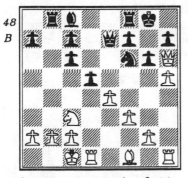

48
B

and now, instead of 14 ...

♕b4 15 hg fg 16 e5 as in Filipjenko - Vorotnikov, Jurmala 1980, when Filipjenko suggests 16 ... ♕xb2+ 17 ♔d2 ♗f5 with interesting play, I think that Black can clarify matters at once with 14 ... ♖xb2! 15 ♔xb2 ♕b4+ 16 ♔c1 ♕xc3 17 hg fg (of course, this recapture is forced here, but time and again in this system, Black recaptures on g6 with the f-pawn. Whilst this is ostensibly anti-positional, its merit is that Black can defend the h-pawn laterally, thereby holding off any crude mating attempts by White. Worth remembering!), when Black has marvellous value for the exchange i.e: 18 ed ♗f5 19 ♘d3 (obviously ♕d2 and ♖d2 both allow ... ♕a1 checkmate; this combination would have been impossible had the white queen been on d2) 19 ... ♕a3+ 20 ♔d2 ♗xd3 21 cd ♕b2+ 22 ♔e1 ♖e8+ 23 ♔f1 ♕e2+ winning.

b) **9 ♗h6!?** (although this move is hardly ever played, I can see no reason for this; White might be able to retain a slight advantage) 9 ... ♗xh6 (9 ... ♘xe4!? is not beyond the bounds of possibility and could appeal to more adventurous players e.g: 10 ♘xe4 ♗xd4 11 ♗xf8

♕xf8 12 c3 ♗g7 13 ♗c4 ♗f5
14 f3?? ♗xe4 15 fe ♗h6∓) 10
♕xh6 ♖e8 11 f3 ♘xd4 12
♖xd4 ♖e5!? 13 ♕d2 (13 f4??
♖h5∓) 13 ... ♗d7 14 g4 ♗c6
15 ♗g2?! ♖e7 16 h4 ♕f8 17
♗f1?! h5! 18 gh ♘xh5 with
good play on the kingside
dark squares, Unzicker –
Keene, Moscow, 1977, but
White wasted valuable time
with his king's bishop.

c) **9 h4** (there is nothing
wrong with this) 9 ... ♘xd4!
10 ♗xd4 ♗e6 11 h5?! (but
there is with this, 11 f3,
would transpose into more
normal lines) 11 ... c5 12 ♗e3
♕a5 13 hg? (this just loses,
which perhaps demon-
strates the danger that
White is exposed to in
Larsen's Variation. 13 f3
was better, although Black
can probably play 13 ...
♘xh5 with the better position) 13 ... ♘xe4! 14 gf+
♗xf7?? (a counter-blunder,
14 ... ♖xf7 would have given
Black's king an important
flight square. Now 15 ♕d3,
pinning the knight, would
have considerably compli-
cated matters) 15 ♘xe4??
♗xb2+! *(49)* 0-1.
J Nielsen – J H Nielsen,
Denmark 1977, 16 ♔xb2
♕xa2+ 17 ♔c3 ♕a3 mate or
17 ♔c1 ♕a1 mate.

        9 ... ♘xd4
This is the thematic
move, but it also possible

to play 9 ... ♖e8 transposing to variation B, or 9 ...
d5?! 10 ed ♘xd5 11 ♗g5! (11
♘xc6 bc 12 ♘xd5 cd 13
♕xd5 ♖b8! 14 b3 ♕f6 is unnecessarily dangerous) 11 ...
♕d7 12 ♘db5 (12 ♘xc6 bc 13
♘xd5 cd 14 ♕xd5 ♖b8 15
b3± is better than before
as the black queen must go
to the less active square
e8) 12 ... a6 13 ♘xd5 ab 14
♘e7+ ♘xe7 15 ♕xd7 ♗xd7 16
♖xd7 ♘c6 17 ♔b1 which
would appear to be to
White's advantage with his
two bishops, and rook on
the seventh. However after
17 ... ♖a4!! 18 ♖xc7 ♖fa8 19
a3 b4 *(50)*

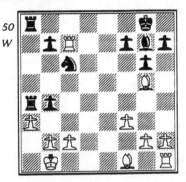

Black has bags of activity and drew, M Gurevich - Zaichik, Lvov 1987.

10 ♗xd4 ♗e6
11 g4

This is the most common move at this stage, and also, in many ways, the most natural. White proceeds with his kingside pawn charge whilst at the same time, being ready to answer ... d5 with g5. The other possibilities are:

a) 11 ♔b1 c5! (this is the key to Black's counterplay in this system, and recurs again and again. Practice has shown that alternative plans are lacking in impetus, for instance: 11 ... a6!? 12 h4 c5 13 ♗e3 ♕a5? 14 ♗h6 - 14 ♕xd6? ♘xe4! - 14 ... ♖fd8 15 ♗xg7 ♔xg7 16 h5 ♘xh5 17 g4 ♘f6 18 ♕h6+ ♔g8 19 g5 ♘h5 20 f4±, Miniboeck - Ermenkov, Vienna 1983. Black could have achieved a more dynamic position if he had played ... b5 on move 13 or 14, and even on move 16 ... ♕c7 in order to defend h7, would have put up more of a fight) 12 ♗e3 (12 ♗xf6 is rarely a serious worry for Black, 12 ... ♗xf6 13 ♕xd6 ♕a5 is already ∓) 12 ... ♕a5 13 ♘d5 (13 g4 returns to the main line; 13 h4 to note 'b'; and 13 ♕xd6?? loses on the spot to 13 ... ♘xe4!) 13 ...

♕a4 (there is no need to play the ending after 13 ... ♕xd2 14 ♘xf6+ ♗xf6 15 ♖xd2 as White will be a tiny bit better) 14 ♘c3 ♕a5 15 a3 (I imagine Black would have been happy with the draw after 15 ♘d5. the onus should be on White to prove he has made something of his extra move) 15 ... ♖fd8 (I don't think that this move is ever really necessary, Black should 'get on with it' over on the queenside, i.e: 15 ... ♖ab8 16 ♕xd6?! ♘xe4 17 ♘xe4 - or 17 fe ♗xc3 18 bc ♖fd8∓ - 17 ... ♖fd8 winning the queen, or 16 ♘b5 ♕b6!) 16 ♗e2 ♖ab8 17 ♗g5 ♕b6?! (Black starts going backwards here) 18 h4 a6 19 h5 ♖d7 20 hg? (20 ♗h6 was better, although Black's resources seem adequate. Heiling gives the variation 20 ... ♗h8 21 g4 ♕c7!? 22 ♕f4 b5 23 ♗g5 b4 24 ♗xf6 bc 25 ♗xh8 ♖xb2+ 26 ♔c1 ♖b1+ 27 ♔xb1 ♕b7+ winning and 24 ♘d5 ♘xd5 25 ed ba 26 b3 ♖b4 27 ♕e3 a2+ 28 ♔xa2 ♕a5+ 29 ♔b1 ♕a1 mate, but White's play here is far from exemplary) 20 ... fg 21 ♕e3 ♖e8 22 ♖d3 d5! *(51)*

When Black was counter-attacking fiercely in the centre, Placketka - Donchev, Bratislava 1983.

b) **11 h4** c5! 12 ♗e3 (Again, 12 ♗xf6? has little merit: 12 ... ♗xf6 13 ♕xd6 ♗xc3 14 ♕xd8 ♗xb2+∓) 12 ... ♕a5 13 a3?! (this is a poor move which weakens the white queenside, a better move is *13 ♔b1* with similar play to the main line, e.g: *13 ... b5!* 13 ... h5? is absurd, the game Prandstetter - Plachetka, Trenchianske Teplice 1985, continuing: 14 ♗h6 ♖fd8 15 ♗g5 ♖d7 16 ♗xf6 ♗xf6 17 ♘d5 ♕d8 18 ♗b5±, why weaken the kingside? *14 ♘d5 b4! 15 ♗h6 ♗xd5! 16 ed ♖ac8∓. 13 ♗h6 is not so bad, either: 13 ... ♗xh6 14 ♕xh6 b5 15 ♗xb5 ♖ab8 16 ♕f4 ♘e8.* 16 ... ♘h5!?. *17 ♗xe8 ♖fxe8 18 ♕f6 ♗xa2 19 ♕xd6 ♗c4* with a mess that soon levelled out in Polowodin - Vorotnikov, Leningrad 1981. I am not so convinced that there is anything wrong with 14 ... ♗xa2 anyway, 15 ♗xd6 ♗e6 leaves White the check on a1 to worry about. What I

do know, though, is that 13 ♕xd6 is still too greedy, 13 ... ♘d7∓) 13 ... ♖fd8 14 ♗g5 a6 15 g4 b5 16 ♔b1? (16 ♗xf6 ♗xf6 17 ♘d5 was perhaps equal, now White's position goes downhill) 16 ... b4 17 ♘d5 ♗xd5 18 ed ♖db8 19 a4 ♘d7 20 h5 ♕xa4 21 ♗c4 ♘e5 22 ♗b3 ♕d7 23 hg ♘xf3 (In his annotations Black gives this move an exclamation mark, but simply 23 ...fg 24 ♕h2 ♗h8 25 ♗a4 ♕f7 looks fine too) 24 gh+ ♔h8 25 ♕f4 ♘xg5 26 ♕xg5 a5 27 ♖de1 ♘e8 28 ♕f5 ♖xe1+ 29 ♖xe1 ♕xf5 (the endgame is very good for Black) 30 gf a4 31 ♗c4 a3 (52)

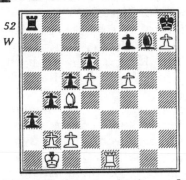

(Black's king's bishop finally gains control of the whole diagonal!) 32 ♖e7 ab 33 ♗a2 c4 0-1, as 34 ♖b7 ♖e8 was Petrushin - Kimelfeld, USSR 1979.

c) **11 ♗e3**. A very intelligent idea; if all Black's play comes from playing ... c5, then why not stop it? Obviously 11 ... c5? 12 ♕xd6

♕a5 13 ♕xc5 would turn into a fiasco but, nevertheless, White has wasted a move and Black should do something soon else his pieces will find themselves 'all dressed up with nowhere to go'. The original game with this move, Chernin – Zaichik, Lvov 1987, continued: 11 ... ♖e8 12 ♗g5 ♕e7 (and not 12 ... c6? because of 13 e5! de 14 ♕xd8 ♖axd8 15 ♖xd8 ♖xd8 18 ♘e4 winning) 13 g4 ♕f8 14 ♔b1 a6 15 h4 when White has a big plus. Although plans involving ... a5-a4 might be feasible, it could well transpire that the simple 11 ... a6 is Black's best, not fearing 12 ♘h6 ♗xh6 13 ♕xh6 ♕e7 14 h4 b5 15 h5 (or 15 g4) 15 ... b4, driving away the white knight and preparing to break open White's queenside with ... a5-a4 and ... b3.

11	...	c5
12	♗e3	♕a5
13	♔b1	

Protecting a2 and preparing ♘d5; the alternative is 13 ♗h6 ♗xh6 (13 ... ♖fd8 14 ♗xg7 ♔xg7 15 h4 h5 16 gh ♘xh5 17 ♖g1 b5 18 ♕g5±, Jurtaev – Gulko, Frunze 1985) 14 ♕xh6 b5 (it is not clear that there is anything wrong with 14 ... ♗xa2, Tseshkovsky gives 15 h4

♗e6 16 h5 with the threat of 17 hg fg 18 g5 ♘h5 19 ♖xh5 gh 20 ♕xe6+, but Black can easily stop this by 16 ... ♖fe8, for instance. The position seems very double edged, but Black might be OK) 15 ♗xb5 ♖ab8 16 ♕f4 (16 ♖xd6 ♖xb5 17 ♘xb5 ♕xb5 18 ♖hd1 ♘d7 19 ♕e3 is a little better for White, although it all depends on whether Black can get his two minor pieces co-ordinated) 16 ... ♘e8 (Unfortunately, 16 ... ♗g7? 17 ♖xd6 ♖xb5 18 ♘xb5 ♕xb5 19 ♕e5! will win the pinned knight by g5) 17 ♗xe8 ♖fxe8 18 ♖xd6?! (18 ♕f6 is better according to Tseshkovsky) 18 ... ♗xa2?! (and now he assesses 18 ... ♖xb2! 19 ♔xb2 ♕b4+ 20 ♔c1 ♕xc3 21 e5 h6 as unclear. After missing this chance Black loses rapidly) 19 ♕f6 ♗e6 20 ♖hd1 ♕a1+ 21 ♔d2 ♕a5 (Black notices that 21 ... ♕xb2? fails to 22 ♖b1 ♕a3 23 ♖xb8 ♖xb8 24 ♖xe6! fe 25 ♕xe6+ ♔g7 26 ♕e5+, forking the king and rook) 23 ♔e3! c4 (and now 22 ... ♖xb2? 23 ♖xe6 fe 24 ♖d7 is curtains) 23 h4 ♖xb2 24 ♔f4! (53)
(The white king heads for the kingside where White has more pawn cover. The absence of Black's king's bishop allows White to

53
B

dominate the dark squares) 24 ... ♖b6 25 ♖d8 ♖b8 26 ♖xb8 ♖xb8 27 h5 gh 28 gh ♖e8 29 h6 ♔f8 30 ♖g1 ♕c7+ 31 e5 1-0 (♖g8+ is unstoppable) Tseshkovsky – Vorotnikov, Atbusbinsk 1985. The whole game looks quite unpleasant for Black and, on reflection, I think that Black should call White's bluff immediately with 13 ... ♗xa2! e.g: 14 ♗xg7 ♔xg7 15 ♕xd6 ♖ad8 16 ♕e5 ♖fe8 17 ♕f4 ♗e6 with powerful threats, or 15 h4 ♗e6 when (an important point!) the white king's flight is blocked by the white queen.

13 ...   b5!

This is the right move here, 13 ... ♖fd8 is too passive: 14 ♗e2 b5 15 ♘d5 ♕a4 16 ♘c3 ♕a5 17 h4 (White is not content with a draw by repetition) 17 ... b4 18 ♘d5 ♗xd5 19 ed ♘d7 (I prefer 19 ... ♖dc8, menacing ... c4-c3, 20 ♗c4 ♘d7-b6 and Black must be at least equal) 20 h5 ♘b6 21

hg hg? (21 ... fg allows Black to defend along the seventh rank) 22 ♗h6 ♗d4 23 ♗g5 ♗g7 (White was probably hoping for 23 ... ♘a4?? 24 ♕xd4! cd 25 ♗f6 which, of course, would not have been possible had Black recaptured on g6 with his f-pawn) 24 ♕f4 ♖e8 25 ♖h7±, as 25 ... ♔xh7? 26 ♕xf7 and ♖h1 will mate, Ernst – Plachetka, Gausdal 1985.

14 ♘d5

The b-pawn is immune from capture: 14 ♗xb5? ♖ab8 15 ♗d3 ♘xe4!∓; or 15 a4 a6 16 ♗d3 ♖xb2+ 17 ♔xb2 ♕b4+, with a swift mating attack. 14 h4 b4 15 ♘d5 ♗xd5 is similar to the game.

14 ...   b4!

This shows the advantage of playing 13 ... b5; Black no longer has to submit to a draw by 14 ... ♕a4 15 ♘c3 ♕a5 etc, but can take the bull by the horns.

15 ♗h6

It is probably wise to exchange Black's dangerous dark squared bishop. If instead 15 h4 ♖ac8 (threatening ... c4-c3) 16 ♗c4 ♘d7 17 h5 ♘b6 18 ♕e2 is already winning for Black in two separate ways: 18 ... ♖fe8!; or 18 ... ♗xb2! 19 ♔xb2 ♕a3+ 20 ♔b1 ♘a4 (or 20 ♔a1 ♕c3+).

15 ...   ♘xd5?

Winning a pawn but throwing away the advantage; better was 15 ... ♗xd5 16 ed ♖ac8 17 ♗c4 ♘d7 18 ♗xg7 ♔xg7 19 h4 ♘e5 20 ♕e2 *(54)*

54
B

and Black might even consider 20 ... f5 here. He has a superb position, the powerful knight on e5 dominating the miserable bishop on c4; Black even holds the upper hand on the kingside, 21 ... fg and 22 ... ♖f4 being one threat.

16	ed	♗xd5
17	♕xd5	♗xh6
18	g5	♗g7
19	h4	♖ae8
20	f4	♕a4
21	♗c4	♕d7 *(55)*

Black's extra pawn is useless and, if anything, it is White who holds the upper hand. The game dribbled to a draw: 22 h5 ♖e3 23 h6 ♗h8 24 ♖hf1 ♖fe8 25 ♔c1 a5 26 ♕xc5 dc 27 ♖xd7 ♖3e7 28 ♖xe7 ♖xe7 29 f5 ♗d4 30 fg ½-½, Zbikowski - Autenrieth, Bundesliga 1985.

55
W

Provided that Black knows want he is doing, the variation with 8 ... ♘c6 appears to be more than satisfactory.

B

| | 8 ... | ♖e8 |

Black by this move, makes sure that he can preserve his king's bishop from exchange, should White play ♗h6. Generally speaking, the play in this section is more complicated than in the previous section, and more pieces are retained on the board. It is perhaps for this reason that 8 ... ♖e8 has proved less popular in practice than 8 ... ♘c6 but, nevertheless, Black's prospects seems quite reasonable.

| | 9 f3 | ♘c6 |

Black can't afford to waste time in such a position, so one would expect 9 ... a6?! to be inferior: 10 ♗h6 (10 g4 b5 11 ♗g5 is not so critical for Black; Joksic - Lehman, Plovdiv 1975, continued 11 ... ♗b7 12 h4 ♘bd7 13 h5?! - 13 ♘d5 is better - 13 ... c5 14 ♘b3 b4 15 hg!? bc 16 gf+ ♔xf7 17 bc, when White has sacrificed a piece for no particular reason. I imagine that a computer would win this position for Black without too much difficulty but, in fact, in the game White managed to make the most of his chances and won) 10 ... ♗h8 11 g4 b5 12 h4 ♗b7 (Larsen analysed several other possibilities here: 12 ... ♖a7?! 13 h5 c5 14 hg! fg 15 ♘4xb5 ab 16 ♘xb5, answering both 16 ... ♖d7 and 16 ... ♖xa2? with 17 ♗c4+; 12 ... b4 13 ♘d5 c5 14 ♘f5 ♗b7 15 ♘de3 ♘xe4 16 fe gf 17 gf ♗xb2+ 18 ♔b1!; and finally, 12 ... c5 13 ♘f5! d5 when, instead of 14 ♘xd5 ♘xd5 15 ♕xd5 ♕xd5 16 ♖xd5 gf which is unclear, Povah points out that 14 ed! b4 15 ♘e4 ♘xe4 16 fe ♖xe4 17 ♕g2 ♗xf5 18 gf is very strong for White) 13 h5 ♘bd7 14 hg fg 15 g5 ♘h5 16 ♖xh5 gh 17 ♗h3 ♘e5 18 ♘d5 ♗c8 19 ♗f5! c6 20 ♘f6+ ♗xf6 21 gf ♕xf6 22 ♖g1+ ♘g6 23 ♗g5 ♕f7 24 ♗xc8 ♖axc8 25 ♘f5 winning rapidly, Povah - van der Weide, 1979. 9 ... ♘bd7 is, however, a possibility, as 10 h4 ♘e5 returns to the main path.

10 g4

10 h4 will probably reach a similar position, but White might try to play h5 without preparation by g4. To date play has proceeded: 10 ... ♘e5! (this is probably the strongest, although Black can try to play as in variation A with *10 ... ♘xd4!? 11 ♗xd4 ♗e6 12 h5 c6?!* 12 ... c5 seems more to the point. *13 hg.* Suetin considers 13 g4 b5 14 ♕h2 to be clearly better for White, but 14 ... b4 seems OK, White is not really going to play 15 ♗xf6? ♕xf6 16 ♕xh7+? ♔f7 17 ♘a4 ♖h8∓ is he? *13 ... fg! 14 ♕g5 ♕e7 15 ♕h4 b5 16 g4 b4 17 ♘e2 c5 18 ♗e3 ♗xa2 19 ♘f4 ♗f7 20 g5 ♘h5! 21 ♘xh5 gh 22 g6!? hg 23 ♕xe7 ♖xe7 24 ♖xd6* with a level ending, Radulov - Uusi, USSR 1970, although Black managed to misplay it and lose. This strange mix of systems deserves to be tried more often) 11 ♗h6!? (*11 ♗e2 a6 12 g4* is the best way to reach the main line, as *11 g4?* immediately allows *11 ... c5 12 ♘b3 ♘xf3* with a rout. *11 ♔b1 a6 12 ♗g5 b5 13 h5 ♗b7? 14 hg fg 15 ♘b3 b4 16 ♘d5 ♗xd5 17 ed ♕b8 18 ♕f4 ♘ed7 19 ♗c4* was all wrong for Black in Hardicsay - Prinz, Boblingen 1985; pre-

sumably neither player noticed *13 ... c5! 14 ♘b3*. 14
♘f5? is pointless if White
has not played g4, 14 ...
gf∓. *14 ... c4 15 ♘d4*. Or 15
♘c5 b4. *15 ... b4 16 ♘d5 c3!*
or *14 ♘de2 ♘c4* with a ter-
rific position for Black in
all cases) 11 ... ♗h8 12 h5
♘xh5 13 g4 ♘g3 14 ♖h3
♘xf1 15 ♖xf1 c5 16 ♘f5 ♘c4
17 ♕d3 ♗e6 18 b3 also worked out well for White in
the game Koronghy - Tor-
nai, Hungary 1972, after: 18
... ♕a5? 19 bc ♗xc3 20 f4
♗xf5 21 gf ♗d4 (21 ... ♕a3+
only loses a piece) 22 fg fg
23 f5 gf 24 ♖g3+ ♔h8 25 c3
♗e5 26 ♗g5! fe 27 ♕xe4
♗xc3 *(56)*

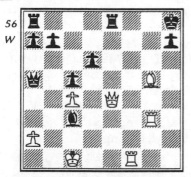

28 ♗f6+! ♗xf6 29 ♕xh7+! 1-0
(29 ... ♔xh7 30 ♖h1+ forces
mate). Black had obviously
misjudged his chances after
18 ... ♕a5, for if he had
played 18 ... ♘e5 19 ♕d2 ♕a5
instead, he would have had
a strong attack (and a pawn
to boot!). Of course, this
would have deprived the

spectators of the beautiful
finish, but I'm sure that
Black wouldn't have min-
ded much.

The other two moves
that have occurred in practice are **10 ♔b1** a6 11 ♘de2
b5 12 ♘f4 ♗d7 13 h4 h5 14
♘cd5 ♖b8 15 ♕c1? ♘h7 16
♕d2 ♘e5∓, Schmidt - Al-
burt, Moscow 1970 (I don't
understand any of this!);
and **10 ♗b5 ♗d7 11 ♖he1**
(else 11 ... ♘xe4 might have
been a problem, as in the
aforementioned game Vyed
- Szabo) 11 ... ♘e5= (or 11 ...
a6 perhaps) Zatulowski -
Kushnir, Match 1971, which
gave Black no problems at
all.

10	...	♘e5
11	♗e2	

Although White probably
would prefer not to play
this move, it is necessary
for the protection of f3
since as before, 11 h4??
loses to 11 ... c5.

11	...	**a6**
12	**h4**	

Larsen, in his book *Why
Not the Philidor Defence?*
published in 1971, also analyses **12 g5** ♘h5 13 f4 (13
♖hg1 b5) 13 ... ♘g4 14 ♗g1
c5! 15 ♘b3 ♗xc3! 16 bc ♖xe4
17 h3 (17 ♘xc5 ♖xe2) 17 ...
♘g3 18 ♗xg4 ♗xg4 19 hg
♘xh1 20 ♕g2 ♕e7 21 ♕xh1
♖e8, with good chances for
Black. Curiously, in the

intervening period, very little of his analysis has had any practical testing. 12 ♗g5 b5 13 ♘d5 ♗b7 14 ♘xf6+ ♗xf6 15 ♗xf6 ♕xf6 is equal, according to Samarian, but why should White want to waste time exchanging pieces like this?

12 ... b5

Larsen, again, mentions that 12 ... c5!? deserves consideration. If 13 ♘b3 c4 14 ♘c5!? ♗xg4 15 ♘xb7 ♕b8 16 ♘xd6 ♘xf3 is good for Black, whilst 14 ♘d4 b5 and 13 ♘f5 will develop along the lines of the main variation.

13 ♗g5

This pin is quite annoying for Black, but it is by no means certain that it is the best move. Others:

a) 13 ♗h6 ♗h8 14 h5 c5 15 ♘f5 (15 ♘b3? c4 16 ♘d4 b4 17 ♘d5 c3!∓) 15 ... b4 (15 ... d5? did not turn out well in the game Tseshkovsky - Lehman, Albena 1977: 16 hg fg 17 g5 d4? - 17 ... ♗xf5 first was better, 18 ef d4 19 gf dc 20 ♕xc3 ♕f6± - 18 gf ♗xf5 19 ♘d5! ♗e6 20 ♗g5! ♗xd5 21 f7+±) 16 ♘d5 ♘xd5 17 ♕xd5 ♗e6 18 ♕xd6 ♕f6 is more analysis of Larsen's, when the threats of ... ♘c4, ... ♘xf3 discovering an attack on b2, or ... gf seem to force 19 g5 ♘d3+ 20 ♗xd3 ♕xb2+ 21 ♔d2 gf *(57)* with a

wild position which might not be at all bad for Black.

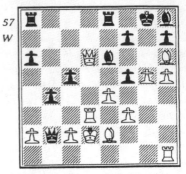

57
W

b) 13 h5 c5 14 ♘f5 (again, 14 ♘b3 invites 14 ... c4 15 ♘d4 b4 16 ♘d5 c3!∓) 14 ... gf!? 15 gf ♔h8 16 ♖hg1 ♖g8, Black should be ready to suffer a little for his extra piece - analysis of Heiling's.

c) 13 ♖hg1 (in order to give added force to the ♘f5 sacrifice) 13 ... c5 14 ♘f5 gf? 15 gf ♔h8 16 ♗h6 winning, but 13 ... b4! 14 ♘d5 c5 15 ♘f5 (15 ♘b3? c4 16 ♘d4 ♘xd5 17 ed ♕a5-+) 15 ... ♘xd5 16 ed ♗xf5 17 gf ♕f6! *(58)* - Heiling.

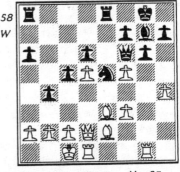

58
W

When 18 ♗g5 ♕xf5 is

winning for Black, and if 18 fg?! then absurd moves like 18 ... ♘g4! are possible.

13 ... c5!?

It is not clear that this is the best move here, 13 ... ♗b7 first might be an improvement: 14 h5 c5 15 ♘f5 (again, forced of course) 15 ... gf 16 gf ♔h8 17 ♖hg1 ♖g8 18 f4 b4! 19 ♘a4 and now, in the place of 19 ... ♘xe4? 20 ♗xd8 ♘xd2 21 h6! ♖axd8 22 hg+ ♖xg7 23 ♖xg7 ♔xg7 as in Sax - Adorjan, Hungary 1971, when 24 f6+! ♔h6 25 fe was much better for White, Black should play 19 ... ♘ed7, when both 20 h6 ♗f8 21 e5 ♖xg5! and 20 ♕xd6 h6 seem to be winning for Black. As it very often happens that Black has the opportunity to take the piece on f5 in this variation, it is interesting to observe how a strong player sets about defending the black position, even if he did err at one point.

14 ♘b3?

As we have previously seen, 14 ♘f5 was obligatory 14 ... gf 15 gf ♔h8 is unclear, but White will have reasonable practical chances. It does of course take quite a lot of courage to put a piece *en prise*; I wonder how many club players would have automatically played 14 ♘b3? Probably

the majority.

14	...	c4
15	♘d4	b4
16	♘d5	c3!
17	bc	bc
18	♘xc3	

18 ♕xc3 allows Black to unpin with 18 ... ♘xd5 19 ed ♕b6 when White must face a powerful attack.

18	...	♕a5
19	♘b3	♕a3+
20	♔b1	(59)

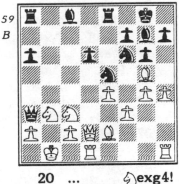

20	...	♘exg4!
21	♕xd6?	

Of course 21 fg ♘xe4 wins on the spot, but 21 e5! allowed White to make a game of it, e.g: 21 ... ♘xe5 22 ♕xd6 ♕xd6 23 ♖xd6 ♗e6∓.

21 ... ♘xe4!! (60)

Superb! Black sacrifices his queen, but wins more than enough material for it and maintains his attack.

22	♕xa3	♘xc3+
23	♔c1	♘xe2+
24	♔b1	

24 ♔d2 is prohibited: 24 ... ♗c3+ 25 ♔d3 ♗f5+ 26 ♔c4

60
W

♘e5+ 27 ♚d5 ♗e6+ 28 ♚e4
f5+ 29 ♚e3 ♘c4+ winning.

24	...	♘f2
25	♖d8	♖xd8
26	♗xd8	♘xh1
27	♕e7	♘c3+
28	♚c1	♘xa2+
29	♚b1	♘c3+
30	♚c1	h5
31	♕e8+	♚h7
32	♕xf7	♗e6
33	♕xe6	♖xd8
34	♘d2	

34 ♕xa6 ♖d1+ 35 ♚b2
♖b1+ 36 ♚a3 lets Black's
king's bishop have the final
word: 36 ... ♗f8+ mating.

34	...	♘g3

0-1

The black pieces are ho-
ming in for the kill, Bengt-
sson - Wahlbom, Uppsala
1970.

If you were to ask me
which is better, variation A
(with 8 ... ♘c6) or variation
B (with 8 ... ♖e8), then I
would have to say: I don't
know. Why not try both?

Although there may seem
to be a lot of variations to
remember, it is really not
so much when you compare
it with, say, the Sicilian
Dragon (I have four books
at home just for the Yugoslav attack!).

Any unprepared white
player will have to find his
way through a veritable
minefield over the board,
and the slightest mistake
can present Black with just
the sort of violent attack
of which he dreams.

6) Antoshin's Variation

1	e4	e5
2	♘f3	d6
3	d4	ed
4	♘xd4	♘f6
5	♘c3	♗e7 (61)

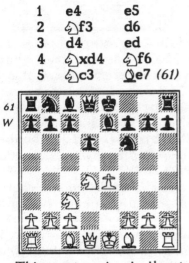

61
W

This system is similar to Larsen's variation in that Black takes on d4 and concedes the centre, but instead of fianchettoing his king's bishop he plays it immediately to e7. Whilst he may not suffer the potential dark-square weakness of Larsen's system, on the other hand, his counterplay will be slower.

Although this variation has been employed by both Morphy and Nimzowitsch, it is the Soviet players Holmov, Georgadze and, in particular, Antoshin who have proved its viability.

Before proceeding with the analysis, I should mention that this position can equally well be reached by 3 ... ♘f6 4 ♘c3 ed 5 ♘xd4 ♗e7, though in this case, Black will have to be conversant with 4 de (chapter 10). In either case ♕xd4 instead of ♘xd4 will transpose to chapter 7.

White's sixth moves are classified as follows:

A 6 ♗f4!
B 6 g3
C 6 ♗c4
D 6 ♗e2
E 6 ♗d3

A

6	♗f4!	0-0
7	♕d2 (62)	

As in Larsen's variation the most critical test of Black's set-up involves the quick mobilization of the queenside pieces and castling long by White. Not only does this threaten to swamp Black with a king-

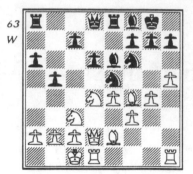

side pawn avalanche, but also the pressure along the d-file will make it difficult for Black to carry out the freeing pawn advance ... d5.

7   ...   a6

By controlling b5, Black prepares either ... d5 or ... b5, but there are several alternatives:

a) 7 ... ♘c6 (this sensible developing move does nothing to stop White from implementing his basic plan of a kingside pawn storm) 8 0-0-0 ♘xd4 9 ♕xd4 ♗e6 10 f3 a6 11 g4 ♖e8 12 h4 b5 13 g5 c5 14 ♕e3 ♘h5 15 ♗h2 ♕a5 16 ♔b1 c4 17 ♘d5, Tal – Holmov. Riga 1968, which was very much to White's advantage.

b) 7 ... ♖e8 8 0-0-0 ♗f8 9 f3 ♘bd7 (Black's play is very slow, and by the time that he decides to start play on the queenside, it is already too late) 10 g4 ♘e5 11 ♗e2 a6 12 h4 b5 13 h5 ♗e6? (63) 14 ♘xe6 fe? (this careless recapture is a

blunder, losing a piece in an amusing manner, but White's attack was well on the way to hitting its target anyway) 15 ♘xe5 de 16 g5 ♗d6 17 gf ♕xf6 18 ♕e3 ♕e7 19 ♖d3 ♖fd8 20 ♕d2 1-0 Kashdan – Koltanowski, London 1932.

c) 7 ... d5!? (indeed, there is a certain amount of logic behind playing this thrust while the white king is still on e1) 8 ed (*8 e5 ♘h5 9 ♗g3 f6*. 9 ... f5 may well be an improvement as 10 e6? would be answered by 10 ... f4; 10 f4 c5 11 ♘db5 d4 12 ♘e2 a6 13 ♘a3 ♗e6 is truly miserable for White; and 10 ef would transpose into the continuation below without allowing White's next alternative. *10 ef*. Keres suggested 10 e6 as an improvement. *10 ... ♗xf6 11 ♗e2 ♗g5 12 ♕d3 ♘f4=* Zuravlev – Golcov, Corr 1968, whilst *8 ♘db5 ♗b4! 9 ed ♖e8+ 10 ♗e2 ♘e4 11 ♕d3 ♗f5 12 ♕f3 ♘a6 13 0-0 ♗xc3.*

Shilov - Podolsky, USSR 1979, is fine for Black) 8 ... ♗b4! (8 ... ♘xd5 9 ♘xd5 ♕xd5 10 ♘b5 ♕e4+ 11 ♗e2 ♘a6 12 0-0 ♖d8 13 ♗d3 ♕c6 14 ♕e3 ♖e8 15 ♖fe1 led to a quick crush for White in the game Kirilov - Darzniek, USSR 1972) 9 0-0-0 ♗xc3 10 ♕xc3 ♘xd5 11 ♕g3 ♘xf4 12 ♕xf4 ♕d5 13 ♘b3 ♕f5 was only a little better for White, Agapov - Antoshin, USSR 1983.

d) **7 ... c6!?** 8 0-0-0 (8 ♗e2 occurred in a couple of games of the Danish correspondence player Granberg in 1984, both continuing 8 ... d5 9 ed ♘xd5 10 ♘xd5 ♕xd5 11 ♗f3 ♕c4, which looks fairly equal) 8 ... b5 (whilst examining these games I noticed that *8 ... d5 seems to be a sensible solution to Black's problems, e.g: 9 ed ♘xd5 10 ♘xd5 ♕xd5 11 ♘b3. 11 ♔b1 c5 12 ♘f3 ♕xd2 13 ♖xd2 ♘c6. 11 ... ♕xd2+ 12 ♖xd2 ♘d7 13 ♗d3 ♘f6 14 ♖he1? ♘d5∓ as any move of the bishop along the h2-g8 diagonal allows ... ♗g5, and 15 ♗e3 ♘xe3 16 fe is awful, so 15 g3 ♗e6 16 ♗e5 ♘b4 17 a3 ♘xd3+ gaining the bishop pair; or 9 e5 ♘e8 10 ♗d3 ♘c7 11 ♘f5 ♗xf5 12 ♗xf5 ♘e6 13 ♗g3 ♘a6, say, with the plan of ... ♘ac7, and ... f6 or ... f5*. Of course, only

a real game could provide a test of all this) 9 f3 b4 10 ♘ce2 (10 ♘b1 has also been played with success, but it must be inferior. The knight is more active on e2, however, Hyldkrog - I Jensen, Corr 1984, continued 10 ... ♕b6 11 g4 d5 12 e5 ♘e8 13 h4 ♘c7 14 ♘f5 ♗c5? 15 ♗d3 ♘d7 16 ♗h6!±) 10 ... ♘h5?! (this seems to be a waste of time, 10 ... a5 might better) 11 h4 (11 g4 ♘xf4 12 ♘xf4 c5 13 ♘f5 ♗xf5 14 ef ♘c6 15 ♘d5± B Christensen - Granberg, Corr 1984) 11 ... c5 12 ♘b5 ♗d7 13 ♘xd6 ♕a5 14 ♕d5 ♘xf4 15 ♘xf4 ♗c6 16 ♕c4 ♘d7 17 ♘f5 when Black did not have enough compensation for his pawn, Charushin - Granberg, Corr 1989.

8 0-0-0 d5

It appears that Black must play this since the alternative **8 ... b5**, fares badly: 9 f3 b4 10 ♘d5 ♘xd5 11 ed a5 12 g4! (12 ♗c4 ♗b7 13 ♘f5 ♘d7 14 ♘xe7+ ♕xe7 15 ♖he1 was also better for White in Holmov - Antoshin, Havana 1968) 12 ... ♗b7 13 ♘f5 ♗f6 14 h4 ♕d7? 15 ♗g5! ♕d8 16 ♖e1 ♘d7 17 ♖e7!! *(64)*

17 ... ♔h8 (17 ... ♗xe7 18 ♘xe7+ ♔h8 19 ♘g6+, winning the queen, is the attractive point of White's tactic) 18 ♖xd7 ♗xb2+ (des-

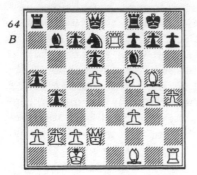

64
B

peration, 18 ... ♕xd7 19 ♗xf6
gf 20 ♕h6 leads to mate) 19
♔xb2 ♕xd7 20 ♗f6 (anyway!
20 ... gf 21 ♕h6 ♖g8 22
♕xf6+) 1-0 Petrosian - Gusev, USSR 1968.

Slower moves, such as **8
... ♖e8** 9 f3 b5 10 g4 ♗b7 11
♘f5 ♘bd7 12 h4 ♘b6 13 h5
Ciocaltea - Vaisman, Ru-
mania 1980; or 8 ... ♘c6 9 f3
♘xd4 10 ♕xd4 ♗e6 11 ♔b1
b5 12 ♕d2 Sveshnikov -
Kalatozishvili, USSR 1975,
cannot be better.

9 ed

In practice this has been
the preferred move, 9 ♘xd5
♘xd5 10 ed ♕xd5 will transpose to a later note, 9 e5
is often given as best here
with the follow-up 9 ...
♘h5 10 ♗e3 c5 11 ♘b3 d4 12
♕e2 ♕c7 13 ♘d5 ♕xe5 14
♘xe7+ ♕xe7 15 ♗d2! (not 15
♕xh5 de 16 ♖e1, Bitman -
Ageichenko, Moscow 1967,
when 16 ... ♕c7 17 ♖xe3 c4
is equal) 15 ... ♕xe2 16 ♗xe2
♘f6 17 ♘xc5 with a clear
advantage to White in the
endgame - analysis by Es-
trin - but I'm not convinced
as 12 ... ♕c7 looks too ob-
liging. 12 ... g6 leaves the
white pieces tangled up: 13
♗h6? loses immediately to
13 ... ♗g5+; and 13 ♘e4 ♘d7
14 ♗h6 ♖e8 is also fine for
Black. Anyhow, 9 ... ♘e8 is
good, when 10 ♘b3 c6 all-
ows Black to develop his
pieces behind his solid wall
of queenside pawns, after
which White will have great
difficulties keeping it re-
strained. It is not easy to
give concrete variations,
but 11 f3 ♘c7 12 ♗d3 c5 is
one possibility; or 12 h4 a5
13 a4 ♘ba6.

9 ... ♘xd5
10 ♘f5!

10 ♘xd5 ♕xd5 11 ♘b3
♕c6! 12 ♗d3 (12 ♗e2 ♕a4 13
♗xc7 ♘c6 gives Black good
play for the pawn, Holmov
- Garcia, Havana 1968) 12 ...
♕a4! (not 12 ... ♗e6 13 ♕e3
♕b6 14 ♕xb6 cb 15 ♗e3±
Liberzon - Antoshin, USSR
1971) 13 ♔b1 ♘c6 14 ♗xc7
♗e6 and ... ♖ac8 when Black
will have a strong queen-
side initiative for the pawn.

10 ... ♘xf4
11 ♕e3!?

11 ♘xe7+ ♕xe7 12 ♕xf4
♗e6 13 g3 ♘c6 14 ♗g2 ♖ad8
15 ♗xc6 bc 16 ♖xd8 ♖xd8
was soon agreed drawn in
Zaitsev - Antoshin, USSR
1969. Obviously 11 ♕xf4??

&g5 is not good, but in his annotations of the above game Estrin analyses the text move and his analysis was later tried out in the (blitz) game Gipslis - Antoshin, Moscow 1972.

11	...	&g5!
12	♖xd8	♖xd8
13	♕e4 *(65)*	

White must defend the knight on f5, since 13 ♔b1? &xf5 14 h4 &h6 hands Black a material superiority to go with his initiative.

13	...	♘e2+
14	♔b1	♘xc3+
15	bc	♖d1+
16	♔b2	&c1+
17	♔b3	&e6+
18	&c4	♘d7!
19	♕xe6 *(66)*	

Forced, as both ♘c5+ and ♖xh1 were menaced e.g: 19 ♕g4? ♘c5+ 20 ♔b4 a5+ 21 ♔xc5 &a3+ 22 ♔b5 &d7 mate.

This weird position deserves a diagram.

19	...	♘c5+
20	♔b4	♘xe6

21	♖xd1

So far, this seems unavoidable. Now various sources give this as either ± or ∓, presumably on account on White's control of the d-file, and his active king. However, at the moment, his queenside pawns are weak and there are opposite colour bishops on the board. I assess this as unclear, e.g: 21 ... a5+ 22 ♔b5 (22 ♔b3?? ♘c5 mate !; 22 ♔a4 ♘c5+ 23 ♔b5 &a3) 22 ... &b2 23 ♖d7 &xc3.

In conclusion, against 6 &f4, which is the most critical move, Black must play ... d5 either immediately on move 7 or after preparation by ... a6 or (possibly best) by ... c6.

B

6	g3

This move has enjoyed a certain vogue of late. White's plan is clear: he intends &g2, taking a firm hold on d5 and making it impossible for Black to free himself.

In the light of this Black plays:

6 ... d5!?

The alternatives: 6 ... ♗d7 7 ♗g2 ♘c6 8 ♘f5 0-0 9 0-0 ♖e8 10 ♘xe7+, Shamkovich - Holmov, USSR Ch 1964/5; and 6 ... 0-0 7 ♗g2 ♗g4 8 ♕d2! ♘c6 9 h3 ♗d7 10 ♘de2! ♖e8 11 b3, Spassky - Holmov, USSR 1971, leave Black poorly placed. It is noticeable that Spassky (who was world champion at the time) assiduously avoids any exchange which would ease Black's task.

7 e5

The only principled reply, Kudrin - Chiburdanidze, Kusadasi 1990, continued instead 7 ed?! ♘xd5 8 ♘f3 ♘xc3 9 ♕xd8+ ♗xd8 10 bc ♗f5 11 ♗g2 ♘c6 12 0-0 ½-½, but White is already worse.

7 ... ♘g4?!

Universally played in this position, but quite possibly not the best, Zaitsev gives 7 ... ♘e4!? 8 ♘xe4 de 9 ♗g2 ♕d5 10 0-0 ♘c6! as equal, and he may be right: 11 ♘xc6 ♕xc6 12 ♖e1 ♗f5 13 ♕e2 0-0-0 14 ♗xe4 ♗xe4 15 ♕xe4 ♕xe4 16 ♖xe4 ♖d1+ 17 ♔g2 ♖8d8 *(67)* would give White considerable problems developing his queenside, as 18 b3 ♗a3

wins. And if instead 14 ♗f4, then 14 ... g5 keeps the equilibrium.

8 ♗f4

8 e6 is very tempting but seems to backfire: 8 ... ♘f6 9 ef+ (9 ♗h3 ♘c6! 10 ef+ ♔xf7 11 ♗xc8 ♕xc8 12 ♘f3 ♕d7 13 0-0 ♖he8 14 ♕d3, Speelman - Georgadze, Hastings 1979/80, when 14 ... ♔g8 15 ♗g5 ♘b4 16 ♕d2 c6 is slightly better for Black. and 11 ... ♖xc8 would be simpler still) 9 ... ♔xf7 10 ♗g2 c6 11 0-0 ♖e8 (11 ... ♘bd7 12 ♖e1 ♘c5 13 b4! ♘e6 14 b5 of Geller - Georgadze, USSR Ch 1979, is unclear, though Black was soon better) 12 ♘ce2 (12 ♗f4 ♘a6 13 ♕d2 ♘c5 14 ♖ae1 ♘e6 15 ♗e5 ♘xd4 16 ♕xd4 ♗f4 is also level) 12 ... ♘bd7 13 b3 ♘e5 14 ♗b2 ♗c5 15 h3 ♕b6= Halifman - Kuzmin, Lvov 1990.

Whereas the risky **8 ♘f3** led to a slight plus for White in the game Palatnik - Holmov, USSR 1972: 8 ...

♗c5 9 ♕xd5 ♗xf2+ 10 ♔e2 ♗b6 11 h3 ♘h6 12 ♕xd8+ ♔xd8 13 ♗g5+ ♔e8 14 h4 ♘g8 15 ♖e1 ♘c6 16 ♔d1 ♗e6 17 ♗b5 ♘ge7 18 ♔c1 a6 although Black shouldn't have too many problems here. However, many players would find 10 ... b6 very tempting here as 11 ♕xa8?? ♗a6+ leads to mate, and 11 ♕xd8+ ♔xd8 12 h3 ♗a6+ 13 ♔d1 ♗b7 14 ♗g2 ♘e3+ also appears very promising. Why it was not tried, I do not know.

8 ... c5

In the game Smirin - Kuzmin, Lvov 1990, Black essayed the ultra sharp 8 ... 0-0?! when 9 h3 ♘xe5 10 ♗xe5 ♖e8 11 ♗e2 ♗b4 12 ♗f4 c5 13 ♘b5 d4 14 0-0! ♗xh3 (14 ... dc? 15 ♕xd8 ♖xd8 16 bc ♗a5 17 ♗c7!+- is the neat point) 15 ♘a4 ♘c6 (15 ... ♕d5 16 ♗f3) 16 ♘d6 ♖xe2 17 ♕xe2 c4 *(68)*

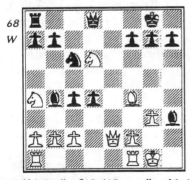

18 ♕h5! ♗xf1? (18 ... ♗xd6 19 ♕xh3 b5 20 ♗xd6 ♕xd6 21 ♘c3 dc 22 bc is Black's best

attempt, although White is still somewhat better) 19 ♕xf7+ ♔h8 20 ♘xb7 1-0. A game of pure complications!

9	♘bd5	d4
10	♘d5	0-0
11	♗g2	♘c6
12	♕e2	♗g5
13	♗xg5	♕xg5
14	f4	♕g6
15	0-0-0	♗e6
16	♗e4	♕h6
17	♘dc7	

This has been on the cards for some time; Black manages to give up the exchange for some tactical play around White's king, but it may not be enough.

17	..	♘e3
18	♘xa8	♖xa8
19	♘c7	♖c8
20	♘xe6	♕xe6
21	♖d3	♘b4
22	♖a3	c4
23	♖xe3	

Wisely deciding to return the exchange.

23 ... c3! *(69)*

No thanks! 23 ... de 24 a3 is clearly better for White.

24 b3

White can keep his rook with 24 ♖f3??, but after 24 ... ♕xa2 he loses his king!

24	...	de
25	a3	

And now the game Deiko - Antoshin, Minsk 1983, terminated in a very strange fashion - presum-

ably due to mutual time pressure:

25 ...   ♘a6??

25 ... ♘d5 seems to hold - 26 ♖d1 ♕e7 or 26 ♗xd5 ♕xd5 27 ♖d1 ♕c5 both threaten ... ♕xa3+ and mate.

26 ♗xb7   ♕e7
27 ♕xa6

This is presumably what Black missed, a3 is defended.

27 ...   ♖d8
28 ♖d1?   ♖d2
29 ♖xd2?   ed+
30 ♔d1   ♕c5

Suddenly Black has some very potent threats that oblige White to make a draw by perpetual check.

31 ♗g2   g6
32 ♕d3   ♕xa3
33 ♕d8+   ½-½

I have to say that the whole game looks very fishy to me, and therefore I should prefer the, admittedly untried, 7 ... ♘e4 to 7 ... ♘g4.

C

6 ♗c4

Although this move is not particularly common at this stage, this position is quite likely to occur from another move order, viz 1 e4 e5 2 ♘f3 d6 3 ♗c4 ♗e7 (the most solid, but see chapter 1) 4 d4 ed 5 ♘xd4 ♘f6 6 ♘c3 and is therefore important to remember.

6 ...   0-0
7 0-0

This is the most natural, but 7 ♗b3 is also sometimes played, presumably in order to avoid any ♘xe4 tricks; 7 ... ♘a6 8 0-0 ♘c5 9 ♖e1 (9 ♕f3 ♘xb3 10 ab c6 11 ♘f5 was also a little better for White in Westerinen - Garcia, Lugano 1968) 9 ... ♘xb3 10 ab ♖e8 11 ♕f3 ♗d7 12 h3 h6 13 ♗f4 ♘h7 14 ♖ad1 ♗f6 15 ♕g3 ♗h4 16 ♕d3 ♘f8 17 ♘f3 ♘g6 18 ♗h2 ♗c6 19 ♘d4 ♘e5 20 ♗xe5 ♖xe5 21 ♘f3 ♖e8 22 e5 ♗e7 23 ♘d4 ♕d7 24 ♘f5 ♖ad8? (It would have been better to acquiesce in playing a slightly inferior endgame: 24 ... ♗f8 15 ed ♖xe1+ 26 ♖xe1 ♗xd6 27 ♘xd6 ♕xd6 28 ♕xd6 cd 29 ♖d1, as now White demolishes the black kingside) 25 e6! fe (70) 26 ♘xh6+! gh 27 ♕g6+ ♔h8 28 ♕xh6+ ♔g8 29 ♕g6+ ♔h8 30 ♖d4 e5 31 ♖g4 ♕xg4 32 hg ♗f8 33 ♖e3 ♗g7 34 ♕f7

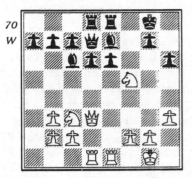

1-0 Diaz - Holmov, Frunze 1989.

The whole idea of exchanging White's light squared bishop seems very time-consuming and leaves White with a nagging space advantage. I think that Black can play more aggressively: 7 ... c5!? 8 ♘de2 (8 ♘f5 ♗xf5 - 8 ... ♘xe4?! 9 ♘h6+ is messy - 9 ef ♕d7 10 ♕f3 ♘c6 is good for Black - ♘d4 is a threat - he has a central pawn and an advantage in development; 8 ♘f3 ♘c6 9 0-0 ♗e6=; but not 8 ♘db5? a6 9 ♘a3 b5 when the white minor pieces look rather silly) 8 ... a6 9 a4 (else ... b5 is annoying) 9 ... ♘c6 10 0-0 ♘b4 taking a firm grip on d5. This type of position reminds me of certain variations of the Sicilian Defence, if Black can keep control over d5 then the disadvantages of the backward d-pawn will be more than outweighed by the dynamic advantages.

7 ... a6!

The obvious 'equalizer' 7 ... ♘xe4 doesn't seems to achieve its objective: 8 ♘xe4 d5 9 ♗d3 de 10 ♗xe4 ♘d7 (10 ... ♘f6 11 c3 ♖e8 12 ♕c2 g6 13 ♗f4 ♗e5? - 13 ... ♘d7± - 14 ♗xe5 ♖xe5 15 f4 ♖e7 16 f5 with a powerful attack, Dvoretsky - Chepukaitis, USSR 1968) 11 ♘f5 ♗f6 12 ♗e3! g6? 13 ♘h6+ ♔h8 14 ♗d5 ♔g7 15 ♘g4 ♔g8 16 ♕f3 ♖e8 17 ♗h6 c6 18 ♖ae1 1-0 Schulz - Alburt, Odessa 1969, but this is hardly model play by Black!

8 a4

In order to protect the white bishop from Black's queenside expansion, but it weakens b4.

8 ... ♘c6
9 ♗f4 ♘b4
10 ♗b3 c5!
11 ♘f3 ♗e6
12 ♘d2?!

A bad move in an uninspiring position, Angantysson - Antoshin, Reykjavik 1976, continued: 12 ... d5 (71)

13 ed ♘fxd5 14 ♘xd5 ♘xd5 15 ♗g3 b5 when Black held the advantage. Antoshin and Georgadze seems to have this system down to a fine art, and it is interesting to compare this with the Mestel - Georgadze game from chapter 1.

D

6   ♗e2

Aside from the more normal 6 ♗f4, 6 g3 and 6 ♗c4, White has a couple of other alternatives. The most important of these is 6 ♗e2, which is a solid continuation, if not particularly troublesome for Black.

6   ...   0-0

There is no reason to delay castling, 6 ...a6 7 0-0 0-0 transposes, and 6 ... d5 is thoroughly inappropriate: 7 e5 ♘e4 8 ♘xe4 de 9 ♗e3±.

7   0-0   c5!

Simple and good. The alternatives are many and varied:

a) **7 ... ♘c6** 8 ♗e3 (8 ♘xc6 doesn't look right, the celebrated game Leonhardt - Nimzowitsch, San Sebastian 1912, continued 8 ... bc 9 b3 d5?! 10 e5 ♘e8 11 f4 f5 12 ♗e3 g6 13 ♘a4 ♗g7 14 ♕d2 ♕d7 15 ♕a5 ♘e6 (blockade!) 16 ♖ad1 ♖d8 and now, instead of 17 ♘c5? when 17 ... ♗xc5 allowed Black to keep his powerful blockade. 17 ♗c5 would have led to White's advantage. As it was, Black won a fine brilliancy. However, Keres indicated that 9 ... ♘d7 10 ♗b2 ♗f6 would have given better chances of equalizing) 8 ... ♗d7 9 f4 ♘xd4 10 ♕xd4 ♗c6 11 ♗f3 ♘d7 12 ♖ad1 ♗f6 13 ♕d2 ♘b6 14 b3 is better for White.

b) **7 ... c6** 8 g4!? d5 9 e5 ♘e4 10 ♘xe4 de 11 ♘f5, again better for White, Myaniskov - Goloscapov, Moscow 1968.

c) **7 ... ♖e8** 8 f4 (8 ♖e1 ♗f8 9 ♗f1 h6 10 ♗f4 ♘bd7 11 h3±, Ioselani - Chiburdanidze, Tel Aviv 1988) 8 ... ♗f8 (8 ... ♘c6 9 ♗e3 ♗d7 10 ♘b3! ♗f8 11 ♗f3 ♕c8 12 h3 b5 13 a3 ♖b8 14 ♖e1 a5 15 ♗f2 b4 16 ♘d5±, Aseev - Kuzmin, USSR Ch 1990) 9 ♗f3 c5 (better than 9 ... ♘a6 10 ♖e1 c6 11 g4!? ♘d7 12 g5±, Abramovic - Franic, Bela Crkva 1987, but 10 ... ♘c5 11 ♘b3 ♘xb3 12 ab± is a better try) 10 ♘b3 ♘c6 11 ♗e3 d5! 12 ed ♖xe3 13 dc ♕b6∞, Smirin - Kuzmin, USSR Ch 1990.

d) **7 ... a6**. This is the most popular, 8 f4 (*8 ♗f3 g6*. Or 8 ... ♘c6 9 ♘xc6 bc 10 ♗f4 ♖b8 11 b3 ♘d7 12 ♕d2 Amirkhanov - Kasparyan, USSR 1956. *9 g3 c5 10 ♘de2 ♘c6 11 ♗g2±*, Tseshkovsky - Georgadze, USSR Ch 1979 and *8 ♖e1 c5 9 ♘b3 b5 10 ♗f3 ♖a7 11 ♗f4 ♗e6 12 ♘d5+-* Tseshkovsky – Georgadze (again!), USSR Ch 1980, are both better for White; but *8 ♗f4* led to a bit more fun for Black in Demetiev – Antoshin, Riga 1970: *8 ... c5 9 ♘f3 ♗e6 10 ♘g5 ♘c6 11 ♘xe6 fe 12 ♗c4 ♕c8 13 ♘a4! ♘xe4 14 ♕g4?* 14 ♘b6 ♕d8 15 ♗xe6+ ♔h8 16 ♘d5± had previously occurred in another Antoshin game, some fourteen years before! Against Ragozin, USSR Ch 1956. *14 ... d5 15 ♘b6 ♘f6! 16 ♕h3 ♕d8 17 ♘xa8? e5! (72)*

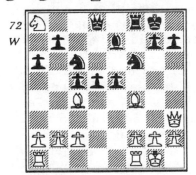

72
W

The black centre sweeps all before it. *18 ♕e6+ ♔h8 19 ♗xe5 dc 20 ♗xf6 ♗xf6 21 ♕xc4 ♕xa8∓.* Finally, *8 a4 c5 9 ♘f3 ♘c6 10 h3 ♘b4 11 ♗g5 ♗e6=* Sakharov – Antoshin, USSR 1967) 8 ... c5 9 ♘b3 b5 10 ♗f3 ♖a7 11 ♗e3 (or 11 a3 ♖e8 12 ♗e3± Forintos – Antoshin, Budapest 1963) 11 ... ♖d7 12 a3 ♗b7 13 ♕e2 ♕c7 14 ♖ad1 ♖7d8 15 g4

and now, instead of 15 ... b4 16 ab cb 17 ♘d5 ♘xd5 18 ed when Black became very cramped on the kingside, Rubinetti – Jimenez, he could have tried 15 ... d5 16 ♘xd5 ♘xd5 17 ed c4 with unclear play. As far as I can see, Antoshin's idea is to provoke a4 by White, when b4 will be weak. However, should White refrain from this, then Black's ... a6 may turn out to be useless; in fact, the weakness of b6 can become a liability. This explains why I have given preference to the immediate ... c5.

e) One last thing: **7 ... d5** is met by 8 ed ♘xd5 9 ♘xd5 ♕xd5 10 ♘b5 when, according to Larsen, Black has a difficult position.

8 ♘b3

8 ♘f5 ♗xf5 9 ef ♕d7 10 ♗f3 ♘c6 is very pleasant for Black, and 8 ♘f3 ♘c6 9 ♗f4 ♗e6 10 ♘g5 (*10 ♕d2 d5 11 ed ♘xd5 12 ♖ad1.* This is better than 12 ♘xd5 which only helps Black's development. In the game Drei – Kosten, Varallo 1991, White was soon in trouble: 12 ... ♕xd5 13 ♕xd5 ♗xd5 14 ♖fd1?! ♗xf3! 15 ♗xf3 ♘d4 16 ♖d2 – of course 16 ♗xb7?! ♘e2+ 17 ♔f1 ♘xf4 is ∓ – 16 ... ♘xf3+ 17 gf ♖fd8 when White was struggling – and ultimately failing to make a

draw. *12 ... ♘xf4 13 ♕xf4 ♕a5*. 13 ... ♕b8 is interesting, if Black can exchange queens then he will have the superior endgame owing to his pair of bishops. *14 ♗d3 ♖ad8 15 ♘g5 ♗xg5 16 ♕xg5 h6 17 ♕h4 ♘d4* is fine for Black, Lowenthal - Morphy, 1st match game, London 1858, remarkably modern play by Morphy) 10 ... d5! 11 ed (11 ♘xe6 fe 12 ed ed is good for Black, his centre and open files compensate the two Bishops, e.g. 13 ♗g3 ♘d4 14 ♗d3 ♗d6∓) 11 ... ♗xd5! (the point, for now, if 12 ♘xd5?? ♘xd5 wins a piece. As it is, White quickly mislays a piece anyway) 12 ♗d3 g6 13 ♘ge4 c4! 14 ♘xf6+ ♗xf6 15 ♗xg6 ♗xc3 16 ♗xh7+ ♔xh7 17 ♕h5+ ♔g8 18 bc ♕f6 *(73)*

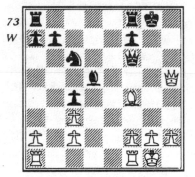

and Black easily warded off the threats and triumphed, Akmentin - Tal, Riga 1954. Obviously, 8 ♘db5? a6 9 ♘a3 b5 would be most embarrassing for White.

8 ... ♘c6

8 ... a6 is also possible, with lines similar to 7 ... a6, but 9 ♗e3 ♘bd7 10 f4 b6 11 ♗f3 ♗b7 12 a4 b5 13 a5 b4 14 ♘d5 ♘xd5 15 ed ♗f6 is an example from this move order, when Black was better, Radzikovska - Markovich, Belgrade 1968. I prefer bringing an extra unit into play if possible. The following is untried, but seems logical to me:

9 ♗f4

Alternatively, White can attempt to discourage Black from playing the freeing ... d5 by 9 f4, e.g. 9 ... ♗e6 10 ♗f3 a5! 11 a4 ♘b4∓ (continuing the fight for d5) 12 ♗e3 ♕b6 (threatening ... ♘xc2!) followed by ... ♖ad8 and ... d5. Should White play f5!? at any time then ... ♗d7 - c6 will pressure e4 and the e5-square will be weak.

9 ... ♗e6

Menacing ... d5 when all Black's worries would be behind him, so:

10	♗f3	♘e5
11	♗xe5	de
12	♘d5	♗xd5
13	ed	e4
14	♗e2	♗d6 *(74)*

The passed white d-pawn is solidly blockaded and his knight has no useful role to play on b3. Also, White's kingside may come under

pressure. All in all, Black is slightly better although this is hardly forced.

E

6 ♗d3

Not a very exciting move. 6 ... 0-0 (6 ... ♘bd7 makes no sense, Herrara - Perdomo, Sancti Spiritus, 1989, continued 7 ♘f5 0-0 8 0-0 ♘e5 9 ♘xe7+ ♕xe7 10 ♗g5 c6 11 f4±) 7 0-0 a6 (7 ... ♖e8 8 ♘4e2 ♗f8 9 ♘g3 c6 10 b3 ♘bd7 11 ♗b2 ♘c5 12 ♕d2 d5! 13 ed ♘xd5=, Yates - Koltanowski, Ramsgate 1929) 8 a4 c5! 9 ♘de2 ♘c6 10 ♘g3 (*10 f4* was treated in interesting fashion by Paul Morphy: *10 ... ♗g4 11 h3 ♗xe2 12*

♕xe2. 12 ♘xe2 ♘b4 13 c3 ♘xd3 14 ♕xd3 d5= Pinder - Boden, Manchester 1857. *12 ... ♖e8 13 ♕f2 ♖c8!* Simple development! *14 g4?! ♘b4 15 b3 d5!*, Barnes - Morphy, 1st match game 1858, for if 16 e5? c4!-+) 10 ... ♗e6 11 h3 d5 12 ed ♘xd5 13 ♕h5 ♘f6 14 ♕h4 ♘e5 15 ♗f5 ♘g6 16 ♗xg6 (forced, as the white queen was running short of squares) 16 ... hg 17 ♗g5 ♖e8 18 ♘ge4 ♘xe4 19 ♗xe7 ♕xe7 (75)

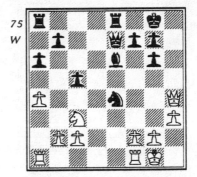

20 ♕xe7?? (this loses material, but 20 ♕xe4 ♗f5 was also better for Black) 20 ... ♖xe7 21 ♘xe4 ♗c4 22 ♖fe1 ♖ae8 0-1, Steinsapir - Romanowski, Leningrad 1940.

7) Morphy's Variation

1	e4	e5
2	♘f3	d6
3	d4	ed
4	♕xd4	(76)

76
B

Although this seems to contravene one of the basic laws of chess, in that the queen is brought into an exposed position in the centre of the board as early as move 4, in fact, as it can be justified tactically, it is perfectly reasonable. Thus the immediate 4 ... ♘c6 can be answered by 5 ♗b5, pinning the knight, 5 ... ♗d7 6 ♗xc6 when the white queen can maintain its dominating position, so Black often defers this move for a time when it will be more effective.

4 ♕xd4 was the preferred move of Paul Morphy (who played it three times in his match against Harrwitz) and Alekhine, in their time and, for what little it's worth, it is also the author's favourite.

Notwithstanding the fact that objectively 4 ♘xd4 is the stronger move, 4 ♕xd4 does have the benefit of avoiding the dangerous intricacies of Larsen's variation, and will therefore have to to be considered by anyone wishing to play this.

I should mention at this point, by way of completeness, that, apart from 4 ♕xd4 and 4 ♘xd4 (which formed the subject of the last few chapters), White can also play the gambit line 4 ♗c4 when 4 ... ♘f6 seems the most sure (although 4 ... ♘c6 was played with success in the game Glek - Dreev, which continued: 5 c3 ♘e5 6 ♘xe5 de 7 ♕b3 ♕e7 8 0-0 c6! 9 f4 b5 10 ♗d3 ♕c5 11 cd ♕xd4+ 12

♔h1 ♗c5 13 ♕c2 ♘e7 and Black managed to surmount his development problems and then take the initiative. Note that 5 ♘xd4 can be well met by 5 ... g6, reaching a branch of Larsen's line which is not at all unfavourable for Black, and 5 ♘g5? meets the retort 5 ... ♘e5) 5 ♘g5 ♗e6! 6 ♗xe6 (but not 6 ♘xe6 fe 7 ♗xe6 ♕e7 8 ♗c8 ♕xe4+ 9 ♕e2 ♕xe2+ 10 ♔xe2 ♘bd7 11 ♗xb7 ♖b8 12 ♗f3 d5 when, despite White's two bishops, I prefer Black; his centre has an improving look and allows the black knights to install themselves on advanced, focal squares) 6 ... fe 7 ♘xe6 ♕e7 8 ♘xd4 ♕xe4+ 9 ♕e2 ♕xe2+ 10 ♔xe2 ♔d7! which looks to be fairly equal.

So, after 4 ♕xd4 we have then the following continuations:

A 4 ... ♘f6!
B 4 ... ♘c6
C 4 ... ♗d7
D 4 ... a6!?
E Others

A

4   ...   ♘f6!

Now there is a further subdivision:

A1 5 e5
A2 5 ♘c3

5 ♗g5 ♗e7 6 ♘c3 will transpose to A2

A1

5   e5!?   ♕e7!?

The Czech Grandmaster, Vlastimil Jansa gives 5 ... de 6 ♕xd8+ ♔xd8 7 ♘xe5 ♗e6 8 ♗c4 ♗xc4 9 ♘xc4 as a little better for White, which may be true, but nevertheless, after 9 ... ♘bd7 10 ♗f4 ♘d5 11 ♗g3 ♗e7 12 0-0 ♗f6 13 ♖d1 c6, say, Black merely suffers from a slightly misplaced king. His position is solid and he should have few problems. He fails to mention, however, what he would have done in the case of 7 ... ♗b4+!, as 8 c3 ♖e8 9 cb ♖xe5+ 10 ♗e2 ♘c6 looks uncomfortable for White as both ... ♘d4 and ... ♘xb4 are threatened, and 8 ♗d2 ♖e8 9 ♗xb4 ♖xe5+ 10 ♗e2 ♘d5 11 ♗d2 ♘c6 also appears to offer Black good prospects. Do note that 8 ... ♗xd2+ 9 ♘xd2 ♖e8 10 ♘df3 ♘d7 pins the knight and relieves White of his problems along the e-line. On top of this, 5 ... ♘g4 may also be playable. Both 6 ed ♕xd6 and 6 ♗g5 ♗e7 seems OK for Black. However practical trials are lacking.

6   ♗e2

6 ♗e3 ♘g4 7 ed ♕xd6 8

♗f4 ♕xd4 9 ♘xd4 c6 is equal, but Black can also try 7 ... cd 8 ♘c3 ♘c6 9 ♗b5 ♘xe3 when he may well be better.

6 ... de
7 ♘xe5 ♘bd7?!

Obvious, but not the best. I think that 7 ... ♕b4+! equalizes comfortably. For instance, 8 ♕xb4 ♗xb4+ 9 ♗d2 ♗xd2+ 10 ♘xd2 ♘bd7 or 9 c3 ♗e7 10 0-0 0-0 and 11 ... ♘bd7 or, finally, 8 ♕c3 ♘bd7 all of which are equal.

8 ♘d3! ♕e4
9 ♕xe4 ♘xe4
10 0-0 ♗d6
11 ♗f3 ♘ec5
12 ♖e1+ ♔d8?

To my mind, a baffling decision; now White's initiative takes on alarming proportions. Is 12 ... ♘e6, masking the e-file, so disastrous? I doubt it. For example: 13 ♘f4 ♘e5! 14 ♗d5 (14 ♘xe6? ♘xf3+ 15 gf ♗xe6∓) 14 ... 0-0! 15 ♘xe6 (15 ♗xe6 fe when Black has the two bishops and the unpleasant threat of ... ♘f3+ and ... ♗xf4) 15 ... fe 16 ♗e4 (this is better than 16 ♗b3 ♘g4! 17 ♖xe6? ♔h8! *(77)*
Black will win the pawn back with advantage, or 17 ♗xe6+ ♗xe6 18 ♖xe6 ♖xf2 threatening mate in two moves, 17 f3 ♗xh2+! and 18

77 W

... ♗g3 is also very strong) 16 ... ♘g4 17 f3 ♗xh2+ 18 ♔f1 ♗g3, Black's position is clearly superior. Therefore, 13 ♘c3 c6= is the best choice.

13 ♘xc5 ♘xc5
14 ♘a3! ♗f5
15 ♗e3 ♘e6
16 ♘b5

And, in the game Jansa - Ermenkov, Prague 1985, White's position was clearly preferable. He went on to win, although not without some difficulty. Like so many games in Philidor's Defence, the stronger player wins, and in his annotations gives the impression that it was a smooth performance from beginning to end. I'm afraid that all strong players are guilty of this to some extent, but as you can see, a close examination often reveals that things are not quite so clear.

Summing up, 5 e5!? leads to equality. Although by its

very nature (releasing the central tension at such an early stage) the ensuing endgames have a drawish look about them, there are still many pieces left and no reason why Black shouldn't try to win.

Remember that as White has the privilege of the first move, nullifying that advantage is a victory in itself.

A2
5 ♘c3

This line has independent signification, as 1 e4 e5 2 ♘f3 d6 3 d4 ♘f6 4 ♘c3 ed 5 ♕xd4 will transpose into this without allowing variation A1 (although, as we've just seen, this doesn't look so terrible).

5 ...   ♗e7
6 ♗g5

This is the most common move at this stage although whilst it does appear the most aggressive, the bishop's position on g5 is slightly exposed and often allows simplification. However, that said, the natural alternative, 6 ♗f4 didn't fare too well in the game Bhend - Tukmakov, Bath 1973, although White's opening wasn't to blame: 6 ... 0-0 7 0-0-0 ♘c6 (by deferring this move till now Black gains a tempo for

development) 8 ♕d2 b6!? (an interesting idea which works surprisingly well, in some lines Black will be able to play ... ♗b7) 9 ♗d3 ♘b4 10 ♘d5 a5 11 ♔b1 ♗e6 12 c4? (12 ♘xf6+ ♗xf6 13 a3 was a better try, since now Black is the first to get things going in his sphere of operation) 12 ... b5! 13 ♖he1 c6 14 ♘e3 bc 15 ♘xc4 d5! 16 ed ♕xd5 *(78)*

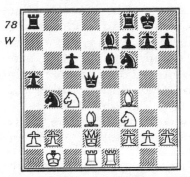

(Now Black wins material) 17 ♘d4 ♘xd3 18 ♕xd3 ♕xc4 19 ♕xc4 ♗xc4 20 ♖xe7 ♘d5, picking up an exchange. Black now managed to steer his way through the complications efficiently to win!

Apart from this, 6 e5?! has been played, although it is of little theoretical value: 6 .. de 7 ♕xd8+ ♗xd8 (of course, Black doesn't have to recapture with his king now) 8 ♘xe5 0-0 9 ♗c4 ♗f5 10 ♗b3 c6 11 ♗e3?! (11 0-0 ♗c7 12 ♘f3 ♘bd7 is more accurate but Black is

still slightly better) 11 ...
♗c7 12 ♘f3 ♘g4! (I have included this game because it
demonstrates how one can
go about trying to obtain
the upper-hand in endings
of this type. As I mentioned
previously, bishops tend to
be rather more effective
than knights in the end-
game, and to possess the
bishop pair can often con-
sititute a decisive advantage. Therefore Black
threatens to exchange one
of his knights for a white
bishop, and at the same
time produce a weakening
of the white pawn struc-
ture; should the bishop
move, probably the better
option, then 13 ... ♖e8+ will
be most inconvenient) 13
0-0-0 ♘xe3 14 fe ♘a6 15
♘h4 ♗g4 16 ♖d4 ♗c8! 17 ♖f1
♘c5 (79)

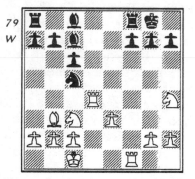

(Ooops, there goes another
bishop!) 18 h3 ♘xb3+ 19 ab
♖e8 20 ♖d3 b5 21 ♘f3? (A
bad move in a bad position)
21 ... b4 22 ♘a4 ♗a6 0-1

Hmadi – Chernin, Tunis 1985.

6 ... 0-0
7 0-0-0 ♘c6

7 ... ♗e6? is completely
illogical, 8 e5! de (8 ...
♘c6?? 9 ef! ♘xd4 10 fe ♕d7
11 ef(♕)+ ♖xf8 12 ♘xd4
brings a whole new mean-
ing to the phrase 'with
compensation for the
queen!' And 9 ... gf 10 ♕e4
fg 11 ♗d3 is even worse) 9
♕h4 ♕c8 10 ♘xe5 with a
strong attack.

8 ♕d2 a6!?

I like the look of this
move, although **8 ... ♗e6**
proved very successful in
the game Ivanovic – Anto-
shin, Sochi 1979: 9 ♗b5!? (9
♘d4 ♘xd4 10 ♕xd4 c5! 11
♕d2 ♕a5 is dangerous only
for White, but 9 ♔b1 is
sensible: 9 ... a6 10 ♗d3 b5
11 ♘d5!? ♗xd5 12 ed ♘e5 13
♘xe5 de 14 ♖he1 occurred
in a rapid game Prie – Kosten, Aubervilliers 1991. Instead of my intended 14 ...
♘d7 15 ♗xe7 ♕xe7 16 f4
♕d6=, I chose first to gain
a move by 14 ... h6?? when
my opponent gleefully
played 15 ♗xh6 as 15 ... gh?
16 ♕xh6 leaves Black wi-
thout a defence to ♖e3 –
g3. So I struggled on
with 15 ... ♘g4 but soon
managed to find some more
blunders to go with this
one and lost) 9 ... ♘b4!? 10
♖he1?! (10 a3 a6 11 ♗e2 ♘c6

must be better, though Black is fine. The plausible 12 ♘d4 is answered by 12 ... ♘xd4 13 ♕xd4 c5 14 ♕d2 ♕a5 and a subsequent b5-b4, when White will be in big trouble. As played, White gets involved in a messy tactical skirmish from which he fails to emerge) 10 ... ♘xa2+ 11 ♘xa2 ♗xa2 12 b3 c6 13 ♗f1 a5 14 ♗xf6 ♗xf6 15 e5 (attempting to exchange queens and block the a1-h8 diagonal, when the bishop on a2 would be lost. Black decides to embark on a policy of opening up the white king's position, whilst keeping queens on the board. Presumably, Black felt that the long-term tactical chances justified this decision, but White misses several good opportunities later on) 15 ... ♗e7 16 ed ♗f6 17 ♘e5 a4 18 ♕b4 ab 19 cb c5 20 ♕b5 ♖a5 21 ♕xb7 c4!? 22 ♘xc4 ♖a8 23 ♖d3 ♖b8 24 ♕f3 (24 ♕c7! exchanges the queens, but Black should be capable of holding the draw. I assume that White was intent on winning: he does, after all, have two extra pawns) 24 ... ♕d7 25 ♖e2 ♕a7 26 ♕e3? (26 d7 had to be tried, when the outcome is still not clear) 26 ... ♕a6 27 ♔d1 ♗xb3+! (wins the exchange)

28 ♖xb3 ♕a1+ *(80)*

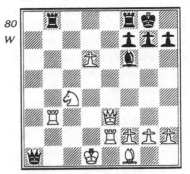

29 ♕c1 (29 ♔c2? ♕a2+ 30 ♘b2 ♖fc8+∓) 29 ... ♕xc1+ 30 ♔xc1 ♖xb3 and Black managed to round up the d-pawn and win.

Apart from 8 ... a6 and 8 ... ♗e6, **8 ... h6** is a reliable alternative: 9 ♗f4 (the overly aggressive 9 h4? just seems to lose a piece to 9 ... hg 10 hg ♘g4 e.g. 11 ♕f4 ♘ce5 12 ♘xe5?? ♗g5-+) 9 ... ♖e8 10 h3 ♗f8 11 ♗d3 ♘e5! 12 ♘xe5 de which is equal, Llorens – Koltanowsky, Spain 1935.

9 ♔b1 b5
10 ♗d3

This reduces the pressure along the d-file, but if instead 10 ♘d4?! then 10 ... ♘xd4 11 ♕xd4 ♗e6 threatening ... c5 and ... b4 or ... ♕a5 could become extremely unpleasant for White as Black's queenside attack gathers momentum very quickly.

10 ... ♘e5!

A common idea in these

lines; if White captures on e5 then the central formation stabilizes, and if not then Black's queenside pawns are free to advance.

11	♘xe5	de
12	f4	c6
13	fe	♞g4
14	♗f4	♝c5
15	♗e2	♛e7 *(81)*

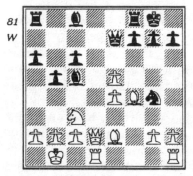

Sax – Tseshkovsky, Banja Luka 1981. Black has a very nice position since the two white e-pawns, are just weaknesses. It seems right, to me, to leave the bishop on c8 for a while and save the tempo for developing the queenside pattern. The bishop might, later on, be more profitably positioned on b7, say. All in all, 4 ... ♞f6 offers the second player good chances.

B

4	...	♞c6
5	♗b5	

This is effectively forced, any queen move would be an admission of defeat.

5	...	♝d7

We have transposed into the Steinitz variation of the Ruy Lopez. There are a number of alternatives:

a) 5 ... ♞e7 6 ♗g5 (6 ♗f4 is less direct) 6 ... h6? (this is not the best way of breaking the pin 6 ... f6 7 ♗h4 a6 8 ♗xc6+ ♞xc6 is much more agreeable for Black and deserves practical tests) 7 ♗h4 ♖g8? 8 ♞c3 g5 9 ♗g3 a6 10 ♗xc6+ ♞xc6 11 ♛e3 g4 (Black tries the utmost to compromise his position) 12 ♗h4 ♗e7 13 ♗xe7 ♞xe7 14 ♞d4 ♖g6 15 0-0-0 ♗e6 16 f4 gf 17 gf ♞c6 18 f4 (persistent!) 18 ... ♗d7 19 ♞d5± ♞xd4 20 ♛xd4 ♗c6 21 f5 ♖g2 22 ♞f6+ ♚e7 23 e5 *(82)*

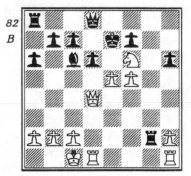

23 ... ♖e2 24 ♖he1 de 25 ♛b4+ ♚xf6 26 ♖xd8 ♖xe1+ 27 ♛xe1 ♖xd8 28 ♛h4+ ♚xf5 29 ♛xd8 1-0 Zuckerman – Bisguier, New York 1969. Not a game that Bisguier would be proud of.

b) 5 ... ♛f6?! 6 ♛d3 ♛g6 7

0-0 a6 8 ♗xc6+ bc 9 ♖e1 ♗e7 10 ♘c3 ♗f6 11 e5!± Bilek - Mestrovic, Albena 1975.

c) **5 ... ♗g4?!** 6 ♗xc6+ bc 7 ♘c3 ♘e7 8 ♗e3 c5 9 ♕d3 ♘c6 10 0-0-0, reaching in a roundabout way, the game Adorjan - Karner, Sochi 1977, where White had slightly the better prospects.

6 ♗xc6

6 ♕e3?! g6 7 ♘c3 ♗g7 is less than nothing for White.

6 ... ♗xc6

6 ... bc is an interesting move. The Yugoslav International Master Basagic surprised me with it at Olot 1990; 7 0-0 (not the best; 7 ♘c3 ♘e7 8 ♗e3 and 9 0-0-0 is more dangerous for Black. Adorjan - Bellon, Lanzarote 1977, went 7 ♘c3 f6 8 ♗e3 g6 9 ♕d2 ♗g7 10 0-0-0 ♕b8 11 ♖he1 ♕b7? 12 e5! with a quick win in sight) 7 ... ♘e7 8 b3 (8 ♘c3 f6 9 ♗e3 c5 10 ♕d3 g6 11 ♖ad1 ♗g7 12 ♖fe1 ♖b8 led to a complicated struggle in the game Mohrlock - Tal, West Germany v USSR 1960 where Black succeeded in coming out on top) 8 ... ♘g6 9 ♗b2 f6 10 c4 ♗e7 11 c5?! (hoping to expose the weak c-pawns, but the plan backfires) 11 ... 0-0 12 ♘bd2 ♘f4 13 ♖fe1 ♘e6 14 ♕c4 ♔h8 15 cd cd 16 ♘d4 ♘xd4

17 ♕xd4 ♗e6 18 ♘c4 ♕c7 19 ♖ac1 a5 20 ♗a3? (20 ♘b6 was better) 20 ... c5! (unexpected and strong: Black devalues his dark-squared bishop, but in the meantime shuts out that of his opponent. The point is that Black's light squared bishop, pressing on d5, becomes a monster) 21 ♕d3 ♖fd8 22 ♘e3 ♕b7 23 ♘d5 ♗f8 24 ♕c4 f5 25 f3 ♖e8 26 ♗b2 a4! (swopping Black's isolated a-pawn off, which at the same time gives White a weakness on b3. At this point I was merely intent on keeping my position from falling apart) 27 ♖cd1 ab 28 ab ♖ab8 29 ♖e3 ♕a7 30 ♗c3 ♕f7 31 ♖de1 ♕h5 32 ♕d3 fe 33 fe ♖xb3?? (33 ... ♗xd5 first was preferable; 34 ed ♖xe3 35 ♖xe3 ♖xb3 36 ♖h3 ♖xc3 37 ♕xc3 ♕xd5 should be a draw, but now Black, anxious to achieve a concrete advantage, and seeing that 34 ♗xg7+ ♗xg7 35 ♕xb3 ♗d4 is good for him, blunders) 34 ♘c7! (of course, this had been impossible previously because of the white queen's placing on c4) 34 ... c4 35 ♕d4 ♖e7 36 ♘xe6 ♖xe6 *(83)*

(In my earlier analysis I had noticed that 37 ♕xc4 was winning - Black will lose the exchange - but it is

83
W

often a good idea that if you see a good move, then have another look to see if there is not a better one. And in this position, there is!) 37 ♖f1 1-0 (if 37 ... ♛e8 38 ♖ef3 or 37 ... ♖e8 38 ♖xf8+ and 39 ♛xg7 mate. There is no point in wasting effort unnecessarily!).

7 ♘c3

7 ♗g5 is accorded an exclamation mark by Ivkov whilst annotating the game Suetin - Damjanovic, Havana 1968. The game continued 7 ... f6?! 8 ♗f4 f5!? 9 ef ♗xf3 10 gf ♛f6 11 ♛e4+ ♚d7 12 ♛xb7 ♖e8+ 13 ♗e3 ♛xf5 14 ♘c3 ♛c5 15 0-0-0 ♛c6 16 ♛xa7 ♘f6 and now White, very sensibly, exchanged queens by 17 ♛a4 and won easily. In fact, it was first played by Morphy and in his 4th game against Harrwitz, in the previously mentioned match, after 7 ... f6?! he continued 8 ♗h4 ♘a6 9 ♘c3 ♛d7 10 0-0 which doesn't look so

wonderful, but Morphy won anyway. In both games. 8 ... ♘e7-g6 must be best.

However, 7 ... f6 is far from being the whole story here. Firstly, the rather surprising move 7 ... ♗e7!? seems to be playable: 8 ♛xg7 ♗f6 9 ♛xh8 ♗xh8 10 ♗xd8 ♗xb2 11 ♗xc7 is probably equal after both 11 ... ♗xa1 and 11 ... ♚d7. 9 ♗xf6 ♛xf6 10 ♛xf6 ♘xf6 will allow Black to regain his pawn, when his bishops might just give him the edge in the calling. In view of all this, in Wade - Dasalov, Tallinn 1971, White tried 8 ♗xe7, yet after 8 ... ♛xe7 he played 9 ♘c3, seeing that 9 ♛xg7 ♛f6 would transpose into the previous note: 9 ... ♗xe4 10 0-0 ♛f6 might also be possible. The follow-up 9 ... ♘f6 10 0-0-0 0-0 11 ♘d5 ♗xd5 12 ed ♛e4 posed few problems for Black. Obviously, the exchange of material tends to help the side with less space which, in Philidor's Defence is almost invariably Black.

For those of you not willing to risk 7 ... ♗e7, 7 ... ♘f6 is also fine. 8 ♗xf6? ♛xf6 9 ♛xf6 gf enfeebles Black's kingside pawns, but leaves Black with the superior minor pieces which, in my opinion, provide more than sufficient compensation. In fact, White is probably worse e.g: 10 ♘c3 f5!? 11 ef ♖g8 12 ♘d4 ♖xg2 or 12 ... ♗xg2 13 ♖g1 0-0-0; or 11 ♘d4 ♗xe4 12 f3 ♗g7 13 fe ♗xd4 14 ef ♗xc3+∓. Instead 8 e5 de 9 ♕xe5+ ♕e7 10 ♗xf6 gf is similarly uninspiring. So 8 ♘c3! returning to the text, has been the normal reply.

7 ... ♘f6

In the game Utjatsky – Suchanow, Moscow 1971, Black essayed the enterprising 7 ... ♗e7!? when 8 ♗d2 ♗f6 9 ♕d3 ♘e7 10 0-0-0 ♕d7 11 ♖he1 0-0-0 was equal. The acid test must be 8 ♕xg7 ♗f6 9 ♕g3 (9 ♕g4 ♗xc3+ 10 bc ♘f6 11 ♕g7 ♖g8) 9 ... ♗xc3+ 10 bc ♗xe4, when 11 0-0 looks a little dangerous, but 11 ♕g7 ♕f6 12 ♗h6? ♗xf3 13 gf 0-0-0 14 ♕xf6 ♘xf6 15 ♗g7 ♖he8+ is better for Black.

8 ♗g5

This seems like an automatic choice, yet **8 b3!?** might be better: 8 ... ♗e7 9 ♗b2 0-0 10 0-0-0 is a little better for White, the queen and bishop lined up on the a1-a8 diagonal looks menacing. In the game Littlewood – Rivas, London 1979, 8 ... g6 9 ♗g5 (change of plans!) 9 ... ♗g7 10 e5 de 11 ♕xe5+ ♔f8 12 0-0 h6 13 ♖ad1 ♘d7 14 ♕xg7+ ♔xg7 15

♗xd8 ♖axd8 16 ♘d4 occurred, and this is assessed as ± by *ECO* C, but 16 ... ♘b8 looks to be equal to me. Furthermore, I don't understand much of this game at all; for example. why didn't Black preface ... h6 by 12 ... ♗xf3 ?

8 0-0 is insipid, yet in the game Adams – Torre, New Orleans 1920, White's apparently mundane play led to possibly the most famous 'sustained overload' combination of all time: 8 ... ♗e7 9 ♘d5 ♗xd5 10 ed 0-0 11 ♗g5 c6 12 c4 cd 13 cd a5? (13 ... h6 would, as we will see later, have given the king a useful loophole) 14 ♖fe1 ♖e8 15 ♖e2 ♖ac8 16 ♖ae1 ♕d7 17 ♗xf6! ♗xf6 (this position appears fine for Black, but ...) 18 ♕g4! *(84)*

18 ... ♕b5 19 ♕c4! ♕d7 20 ♕c7! ♕b5 21 a4! ♕xa4 22 ♖e4 ♕b5 23 ♕xb7! 1-0. Marvellous.

8 ... ♗e7

9   0-0-0

9 0-0 is again possible, but does not really offer White too much: 9 ... h6 10 ♗h4 0-0 11 ♖fe1 ♖e8, Meiklejohn - Sax, Groningen 1972, looks fairly level.

9   ...   0-0

9 ... h6 is generally queried on account of the game Pokojowczyk - Sarwinski, Poland 1976, the difference between this and the main line being that the bishop will be on h4 instead of g5, where, in the following line, it would have been taken with check. The game continued: 10 ♗h4 0-0 11 ♖he1 ♖e8? (11 ... ♘d7 12 ♗xe7 ♕xe7 13 ♘d5± is certainly better) 12 e5! de 13 ♕c4 ♘d7? (13 ... ♗d6!) 14 ♘xe5 (sic) 14 ... ♘xe5 15 ♖xe5 ♗xh4 16 ♖xd8±.

10   ♖he1

Bronstein makes the interesting remark that in this position he can never decide whether to play 10 ♖he1 or to defend the bishop with 10 h4 to be 'on the safe side'. I think that the text is best but, indeed, Alekhine himself played 10 h4 against Mideno, Holland 1933: 10 ... h6 11 ♘d5?! (brilliant but flawed) 11 ... hg 12 ♘xe7+ ♕xe7 13 hg ♘xe4 14 ♖h5 ♕e6? (Larsen points out that by playing 14 ... f5! first, 15 g6 ♕e6 16 ♘e5 ♖fe8

- 16 ... de? would transpose to the game - 17 ♖dh1 ♔f8 18 ♖h8+ ♔e7 19 ♘xc6+ ♔d7!, Black would be better) 15 ♖dh1 f5 16 ♘e5! de 17 g6! *(85)*

1-0. For if 17 ... ♕xg6 18 ♕c4+ and ♖h8 mate, or 17 ... de 18 ♖h8 mate. I can't help thinking that 10 ... h6 is a bit too provocative all the same, 10 ... ♖fe8 is more sensible, and if 11 ♖he1 *then* play 11 ... h6.

10   ...   ♖e8

Other ideas involving the exchange of the dark-squared bishops are worse: 10 ... ♘d7 11 ♗xe7 ♕xe7 12 ♘d5! ♗xd5 13 ed ♕f6 14 ♕e3±, Andersson - Kadiri, Siegen Olympiad 1970; White owns the e-file and can play ♕e7 at a judicious moment. 13 ... ♕d8 14 ♖e3 ♖e8 15 ♖xe8 ♕xe8 16 ♖e1 amounts to the same.

10 ... h6 11 ♗h4 ♘e8 12 ♗xe7 ♕xe7 13 e5?! of Morphy - Harrwitz, 2nd match game and 10 ... ♘e8 11 ♗xe7

Qxe7 12 Qc4 Qe6 of Anderssen (no relation!) - Meitner, Vienna 1873, should both be treated the same way respectively by 13 Nd5 and 12 Nd5 i.e: 12 ... Bxd5 13 ed Qd7 14 Re3 Nf6 15 Rde1 Rfe8 16 Rxe8+ Rxe8 18 Rxe8+ Qxe8 18 Qxa7± (although 13 Qd2 and 14 Nd4, suggested by Morphy in his game, is also worthy of consideration).

11 Kb1

A useful prophylatic move. The immediate 11 e5? is not good: 11 ... de 12 Qc4 Nd7 wins a pawn as 13 Nxe5? Nxe5 14 Rxe5 Bxg5 is check.

11 ... Bd7?

Not a very good move. Black, seeing that the bishop is not particularly useful on c6, decides to reposition it on e6 or g4. However, Black cannot afford such luxuries in this position. 11 ... a5?! is also out of place here, but in the game Parma - S Nikolic, Novi Travnik 1969, White impulsively tried to immediately refute it with 12 e5?! de 13 Qc4 and now, instead of 13 ... Nd7? 14 Nxe5 Nxe5 15 Rxe5 Bxg5 16 Rxd8 Raxd8 17 Rxe8+ Rxe8 18 a4 when White had a clear advantage, although Black later managed to set up a fortress position and draw,

it would have been better to have played 13 ... Qd6 14 Nxe5 Bxe5 15 Rxd8 Raxd8 which offers more compensation for the queen.

From my analysis, there are two alternative moves which deserve consideation here:

a) **11 ... h6!?** would appear to be a useful move, relieving Black of any later back-rank problems at no cost in time, 12 Bh4 and now 12 ... Qd7 is possible, with the intention of continuing ... Qg4, as 13 Bxf6? Bxf6 14 e5 Bxf3 15 gf allows 15 ... Rxe5 16 Rxe5 Qc6! 17 f4 (what else?) 17 ... de 18 fe Rd8 19 Qe3 Rxd1+ 20 Nxd1 Qd5 (21 ... Qxe5).

b) Apart from this, I wonder if **11 ... Qb8!?** (or 12 ... Qb8 after 11 ... h6) is acceptable, the idea being to continue ... b5 and ... Qb7, starting active operations on the queenside: pressing on e4; and at the same time removing the queen from the exposed central file. Now e5 can always be met by ... de or ... Bxf3, as circumstances permit, and Nd5 by ... Nxd5. ... Bxh4 and ... Bd7 with simplification.

12 Bxf6!

This little combination assures White of lasting strategical superiority.

12	...	♗xf6
13	e5	♗e7
14	♘d5	♗f8
15	ed	ed

Obviously, if 15 ... ♗xd6, 16 ♘xc7 wins a pawn, but this may well have been the best way to proceed e.g. 16 ... ♖xe1 17 ♘xe1 ♕xc7 18 ♕xd6 ♕xd6 19 ♖xd6 ♗c6 and 20 ... ♖e8 with some chances to make a draw. As played, the bishop spends almost the entire game passive on f8, completely dominated by White's enormous knight on d5.

16	♖xe8	♗xe8
17	♘d2!	♗c6
18	♘e4	f5
19	♘ec3	♕d7
20	a3	♕f7
21	h3	a6
22	g4	♖e8
23	f4	♖e6

Black defends the f6 square with a view to playing g6, but White has other ideas.

24	g5!	b5
25	h4	♖e8
26	♕d3	♖b8
27	h5	a5

Desperately searching around for counterplay, but White just keeps turning the screw.

28	b4!	ab
29	ab	♕xh5
30	♕xf5	♕f7
31	♕d3	♗d7
32	♘e4	♕f5

33	♖h1	♖e8

33 ... ♔h8 would have avoided the worst, but 34 ♘e3 ♕g6 35 ♖f1, menacing f5, would have kept up the pressure. Finally, after playing a fine strategical game, White rounds it off with a display of tactics for which he was so justly famous.

34 ♘ef6+! *(86)*

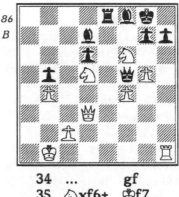

86
B

34	...	gf
35	♘xf6+	♔f7
36	♖xh7+	♗g7
37	♖xg7+	♔xg7
38	♘xe8+	♔f8
39	♕xf5+	♗xf5
40	♘xd6	

Winning easily; Anderssen - L Paulsen, Vienna 1873.

C

4	...	♗d7

The advantage of this move is that Black will immediately drive the white queen from d4 by ... ♘c6. The disadvantage is that the bishop seems poorly placed on d7 in comparison with say, variation A2, where it could go to the more active square e6, g4 or even b7 in one bound.

5 ♗f4

In this case **5 ♗g5?** achieves nothing: 5 ... ♘c6 6 ♕d2 (6 ♗xd8 ♘xd4 - threatening ♘xc2+ - 7 ♘xd4 ♖xd8 is better for Black: two bishops. Incidentally, I can see no reason why all the sources give 7 ... ♔xd8 in this position, as 8 ♘b5 can be answered by 8 ... c6 anyway, and the knight must retreat, or be lost. 6 ♕c3 f6 7 ♗h4 d5! - hoping to play ... ♗b4 - 8 ♕e3 de 9 ♕xe4+ ♗e7 and 0-0-0∓ - the white bishop is misplaced on h4) 6 ... ♗e7 7 ♗xe7 ♕xe7 8 ♘c3 ♘f6 solves most of Black's problems. A game Biyiasas - Smyslov, Bor 1980, continued: 9 0-0-0 0-0-0 10 ♗d3 ♖fe8 11 ♖fe1 ♘e5 12 ♘d4 ♘xd3+ 13 cd?! ♕e5! 14 ♘f3 ♕a5 15 h3 ♗e6 16 ♔b1 d5 17 e5 d4! 18 ef dc∓.

5 ♗e3 will be similar to 5 ♗f4; 5 ... ♘c6 6 ♕d2 ♘f6 7 ♘c3 ♗e7 8 0-0-0 0-0± (8 ♗c4 ♘e5 9 ♘xe5 de 10 0-0 0-0 transposes into a game Morphy - Lowenthal, match 1858; it appears fairly level though White lost).

5 ... ♘c6
6 ♕d2 ♗e7

The Finnish Grandmaster Heikki Westerinen experimented with the move 6 ... ♘ge7 against Kurajica, Solingen 1974, which continued 7 ♘c3 ♘g6 8 ♗g5 ♗e7 9 ♗xe7 ♕xe7 10 0-0-0, but after 10 .... 0-0? it all went wrong: 11 h4 (now the knight will find itself awkwardly placed on g6) 11 ... ♗e6 12 h5 ♘ge5 13 ♘h4! ♖ae8 14 f4 ♘c4 15 ♗xc4 ♗xc4 16 h6 g6 17 b3 ♗a6 18 ♘d5 ♕d8 19 ♕c3 f6 20 ♖he1 ♖f7 21 ♘f3 ♖ef8 22 g4 ♘b8 23 g5 (White has a bone-crushing initiative) 23 ... fg 24 ♘xg5 c6 25 ♘xf7 ♖xf7 26 ♘e3 ♕f8 27 ♘f5! *(87)*

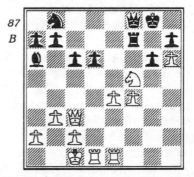

87
B

27 ... ♘d7 (there is the nice point that if 27 ... d5 28 ed ♖xf5 29 ♖e8 wins) 28 ♖xd6 ♘f6 29 ♕d2 and Black threw in the towel, 1-0 (29 ... gf 30 ♖g1+ ♔h8 21 ♖d8 ♘e8 32 ♕d4+ is a likely finish).

7 ♘c3

In the game Blackburne - Deacon, Paris 1862, 7 ♗c4

♘f6 8 ♘c3 0-0 9 0-0?! occurred, and now Black played 9 ... ♘g4! disregarding the d5 square but instead hastening to control e5. White's initiative will be somewhat dulled if there is no threat of e5, levering open the central files. Now 10 ♖ad1 ♗f6 11 ♖fe1 ♘ge5 12 ♗xe5 ♗xe5 13 h3 ♗e6 was perfectly respectable for Black, but 9 0-0-0 is more pointed.

7	...	♘f6
8	0-0-0	0-0
9	h3!	

In my opinion this must be the most accurate, 9 e5?! de 10 ♘xe5 ♘xe5 11 ♗xe5 ♗c6 (*11 ... ♗e6. But not 11 ... ♗g4 12 f3 ♕xd2+ 13 ♖xd2 as Black loses his c-pawn. 12 ♕f4 ♘d7 also seems OK for Black as 13 ♕g3. Obviously 13 ♗xc7?? ♗g5 14 ♗xd8 ♗xf4+ is not recommended for White! 13 ... ♗f6 seems to successfully exchange pieces e.g: 14 ♗xf6 ♕xf6 15 ♕xc7 ♕xf2 16 ♖xd7? ♗xd7 17 ♕xd7 ♖ad8 wins, or 14 ♗f4 ♗h4. And 12 ♕xd8 ♗xd8= 13 ♘b5 ♖c8 14 ♘xa7? ♖a8, followed by ... ♖xa2) 12 ♕f4 ♕c8 13 h3 (it turns out that the threat to c7 is illusory: 13 ♗xc7 ♘h5 14 ♕e5 ♗f6 15 ♕xh5 ♕xc7 is too dangerous for White) 13 ... a6 14 ♗c4 b5 15 ♗xf6 ♗xf6 16 ♗d5 ♗xd5 17 ♘xd5* ♗d8 (*88*) which looks equal but led to a comfortable Black win in Matulovic - Tringov.

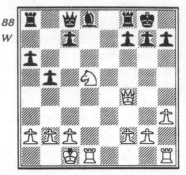

88
W

It has to be remembered that with 9 e5?! White is starting the complications before he has even developed his kingside.

9 ♗d3 is a sensible move but Black might be able to simply play 9 ... ♘g4, getting a firm grip on the e5 square. 10 ♘d5 ♘ge5 11 ♘xe7+ ♕xe7 is a plausible continuation when White has the two bishops, but in this position that may not mean a great deal. Play can continue 12 ♗g5 f6 13 ♗h4 ♗e6 or 13 ... ♗g4 with a reasonable position. Black can consider starting a queenside attack, or he can simply play rooks to e8 and d8. If White captures on e5 then Black can recapture with the d-pawn and utilize the d-file. 9 ... ♘b4 is also possible.

The text 9 h3! is a sugg-

estion of Grandmaster Ku-
rajica's. White takes time
out to stop ... ♘g4 or ...
♗g4 and prepares to play
♗d3 and ♖he1, or perhaps
g4, gaining space on the
kingside. Black's most
promising line of action
appears to be 9 ... ♗e6, with
the further plan to play ...
♘d7, ... ♗f6, and ... ♘de5.
White does not have time
for 10 ♘g5 ♘d7?! 11 ♘xe6 fe
12 ♗c4?? because of 12 ...
♖xf4 and ... ♗g5, but 12 ♗e3
♘de5 13 f4 ♘g6 – menacing
♘xf4 – 14 g3 and White is
better. There is, however,
no good reason to allow
♘xe6; therefore 10 ... ♗c8!
followed by ... h6 and ...
♗e6. In any case, it is clear
that White's space advan-
tage and possibilities of
direct action offer him the
better prospects.

D

4 ... a6

Whilst this move has the
same laudable motive as
variation C, namely to ex-
pel the white queen from
its central postion without
allowing the ♗b5 pin, its
advantage is that queenside
counterplay will come that
much sooner, as ... b5 is
already prepared.

5 ♗f4

Again, 5 ♗g5 is mistaken;
5 ... ♘c6 6 ♕d2 (6 ♗xd8

♘xd4 7 ♘xd4 ♔xd8 8 ♗c4
♘h6, when the black posi-
tion is solid and he has the
bishop pair. He will follow
up with ... g6 and ... ♗g7 or
... ♗e7-f6) 6 ... ♗e7 7 ♘c3
(7 ♗xe7 ♕xe7 8 ♘c3 ♘f6=)
7 ... ♗xg5 8 ♘xg5 and in the
game Sznapik – Plachetka,
Trnava 1984, Black played
the careless 8 ... ♘f6?!
when after 9 f4 0-0 10
0-0-0 White had some ad-
vantage, although the game
later dissolved into a wild,
tactical melee: 10 ... h6 11
♘f3 b5 12 ♗d3 b4 13 ♘d5 a5
14 ♖hg1 ♗e6 15 g4 ♘xd5 16
f5!? ♘c3 which is worth a
diagram, in my view *(89)*

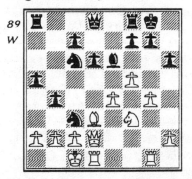

And the game staggered
on: 17 bc ♗xa2 18 g5 hg 19
♖xg5 ♕f6 20 ♖dg1 ♖fb8 21
♖xg7+ when White was
winning although the game
was later drawn. But, of
course, simply 8 ... h6! 9
♘f3 ♘f6 10 0-0-0 0-0,
when the absence of one
pair of pieces eases any
sensations of cramp that

Black might feel in this variation.

5	...	♘c6
6	♕d2	♘f6
7	♘c3	♗e7
8	0-0-0	0-0
9	♗d3	

One advantage of not having the bishop on d7 (as in variation C) is that 9 e5 has absolutely no point here: 9 ... de 10 ♘xe5 ♘xe5 11 ♗xe5 ♕xd2+ 12 ♖xd2 c6=. Also 9 h3 is irrelevant as Black can always play his king's knight to e5 via d7 if he so wishes.

9	...	♘d7

9 ... ♘b4 is not without point here, if White tries to preserve his light-squared bishop by 10 ♗e2 then 10 ... ♗e6 11 a3 a5!? could be fun, as now 12 ab is extremely risky due to 12 ... ab 13 ♘b1 ♖a1 14 ♕xb4 ♗a2 15 ♔d2 d5 *(90)* with a vicious attack.

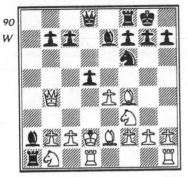

90
W

10 ♗c4?! is met by 10 ... b5.

10	♘d5	♘de5?

Matulovic suggests that 10 ... ♘c5 is best, and he is probably right. If Black manages to take on d3 and then play ... ♗e6 he should be fine.

11	♗e2	♖e8

And here 11 ... ♗e6 looks more sensible to me.

12	♘xe5	♘xe5

Probably overlooking White's next; 12 ... de 13 ♗e3 ♗e6 (but not 13 ... ♗d6? 14 ♘b6!) is only slightly disadvantageous for Black.

13	♕a5!	c6

Not 13 ... b6? 14 ♕c3.

14	♘xe7+	♕xe7
15	♖he1	f6
16	♕a3	♖d8
17	♗g3	♘f7
18	♗f1	c5
19	f4	

When White was clearly better but soon ran short of time, and so decided to offer a draw a few moves later which, of course, was accepted; Matulovic - Barlov, Vrnjacka Banja 1983.

E Other Black fourth moves

a) 4	...	♗g4

A rarely played move, but on the evidence of the game Archvadze - Chipukaitis, USSR 1968, perhaps not so bad:

5	♗g5	♕d7
6	♘c3	

Harding feels that 6 ♘bd2 ♘c6 7 ♕c3 is more consistent, and it does certainly make things more difficult for Black.

	6	...	♞c6
	7	♛d2	♝e7
	8	♝b5	a6
	9	♝e2	♞f6
	10	h3	♝h5
	11	♝e3	♝g6

White's moves appear to be a little purposeless, and following 12 ♝d3 0-0 13 ♛e2 ♖ae8 14 0-0-0 ♝d8! 15 ♞d2 b5 16 a3 d5! Black has assumed the initiative, and went on to win.

b)   4   ...   ♝e6

Lowenthal - Morphy, 7th match game 1858 continued 5 ♞c3 a6 6 ♝e3? ♞c6 7 ♛d2 ♞f6 8 ♖d1 ♝e7 9 ♝e2 0-0 10 0-0 b5= but White's play was not, by any stretch of the imagination, a critical test.

Whilst all these variations are certainly playable for Black, variation A seems the best variation and variation D is also interesting but, to my mind, variations B and C suffer from the fact that the light-squared bishop is not so well placed on, respectively, c6 and d7. Of the other two ideas, 4 ... ♝g4 might be worth a try.

8) Hanham Variation (Improved) Introduction

1	e4	e5
2	♘f3	d6
3	d4	♘f6
4	♘c3	

4 de is discussed in chapter 10, and other assorted moves in chapter 11.

4	...	♘bd7 *(91)*

91
W

This is the key move of this system, although when the American Master Major Hanham originally conceived the plan he played ... ♘d7 on move three. Now we know that this particular order of moves is inferior (see chapter 2), and it was the great chess thinker Aron Nimzowitsch who first introduced the interpolation 3 ... ♘f6 and only then 4 ... ♘bd7.

Black defends his e-pawn and prepares to develop the rest of his pieces, whilst keeping the centre closed. His position, though a little cramped, is solid and without weaknesses. Furthermore, White must take care, as after a moment's carelessness on his part the black pieces can spring to life.

In the main line, which we will look at later, Black can play a patient maneouvering game if he so wishes, but perhaps the best chances are offered by playing a well-timed ... ed and then pressurizing the white e-pawn. It was, again, Nimzowitsch who first showed the possibilities inherent in this strategy of restraint.

5 ♗c4

This is almost invariably played, but there are many alternatives.

a) 5 ♗g5 ♗e7 6 ♕d2?! occurred in a game Wagner – Holzhausen, 1926, when it would appear that 6 ... h6!

is strong, as 7 Be3 is met by 7 ... Ng4 and 7 Bh4? is even worse because of 7 ... Nxe4! 8 Nxe4 Bxh4 (winning a pawn with a better position) or 8 Bxe7 Nxd2 9 Bxd8 Nxf3+ when White can happily resign. So 7 Bxf6 seemed forced, and after 7 ... Bxf6 and Black has every reason to feel contented.

b) **5 Be2 Be7** (as per the main line, but as Black has no worries about his f-pawn, he could just as easily consider playing 5 ... g6 6 0-0 Bg7 with a favourable position for the Pirc) 6 0-0 (6 a4 a5 first, then 7 0-0 0-0 8 Re1 c6 9 b3 Re8 10 Bb2 Bf8= Reicher - Quinteros, Wijk aan zee 1973, but simply 6 ... c6 7 0-0 0-0 8 Re1 Qc7 9 b3 Re8 10 Ba3 Bf8 11 h3 g6 12 de de 13 Bxf8 Nxf8 14 Qd2 Ne6 15 Rad1 Rd8 of Arakhamia - Rogers, Moscow 1989 is also good, with Black gradually assuming the initiative) 6 ... 0-0 (or, more aggressively, 6 ... c6 7 Re1 h6 8 h3? Qc7 9 Be3 g5, Voitcekhovsky - Tartakower, Yuptata 1937) 7 Re1 c6 8 a4 b6 9 b3 a6 10 Bb2 Bb7 11 Bf1 b5 (an interesting position, Black is expanding on the queenside and White is hoping to target Black's e-pawn) 12 de de 13

ab ab (13 ... cb!?) 14 Rxa8 Bxa8 15 Qa1! Re8 16 g3 Bc5 17 Bh3 Bb7 18 Rd1 Bc8 19 Ne2? (White's patience snaps, but 19 Rd2 Qc7 is fine for Black) 19 ... Nxe4 20 Bxd7 Nxf2! 21 Qxe8 Nxd1+ 22 Bd4! ed 23 Bxf7+ Kxf7 24 Qxd1∓ Manca - Kosten, Varallo 1991.

c) **5 de** is a mistake, White hereby releases the tension in the centre and invites the black king's bishop to take up a more than normally active position. Akopjan - Sergievsky, USSR 1964, continued: 5 ... de 6 Bc4 Bb4 (sic) 7 0-0 0-0 8 Nd5 Nxd5 9 Bxd5 c6=.

d) **5 g3** is the only move (apart from 5 Bc4, of course) to have any sort of reputation, indeed Korchnoi himself once played it: 5 ... Be7 (apart from this 'pure Hanham' approach, Black can also play 5 ... g6 6 Bg2 Bg7 reaching another position from the Pirc where, this time, the white knight is misplaced on f3 - it would normally be on e2. One example: 7 0-0 0-0 8 de de 9 b3 b6 10 a4 Bb7 11 Nd2 Re8 12 Ba3 Bf8 13 Bxf8 Nxf8 14 Nc4 Ne6=, Smyslov - Sax, Tilburg 1979) 6 Bg2 0-0 (the game Hebden - Salem, Hastings Open 1991, continued in curious fashion: 6 ... h5!? 7 h3 c6 8 a4 a5 9 b3 ed 10 ♕xd4 ♘c5 11 ♗b2 ♗e6 12 ♖ad1 ♕c7 13 ♕e3 0-0-0 14 ♘d4 ♖he8 15 ♘xe6 fe 16 h4 d5 17 ♕e2 ♘g4 18 ♗h3 ♗f6 19 ♗xg4 hg 20 ♕xg4 ♘xe4 21 ♘xe4 ♗xb2 (92) which is unclear, the game was later drawn after some wild fluctuations)

7 0-0 (from a slightly different move order, the game Kaplan - Panno, Sao Paulo 1973, reached the position after 7 a4 c6 8 a5, and then continued: 8 ... ♕c7 9 0-0 ♕b8! 10 b3 ♖e8 11 ♗b2 b5 12 ab ab 13 ♕e2 ♗b7 14 ♖xa8 ♗xa8 15 ♖d1 b5 with equality, though Black later went on to win) 7 ... c6 8 a4 (probably more accurate than 8 b3 ♖e8 9 ♗b2 of Tartakower - Kostic, Teplitz Shonau 1922) 8 ... ♖e8 9 b3 (or first 8 ♖e1 ♗f8 10 b3, but it is a mistake to give up the centre at this point by 10 ... ed?! 11 ♘xd4 d5 12 ed ♖xe1+ 13 ♕xe1 ♘xd5 14

♘xd5 cd±, Korchnoi - Guimard, Buenos Aires 1960) 9 ... ♗f8 10 ♗b2 ♕c7 11 ♖e1 b6 12 ♘h4 ♗b7= Hase - Rubinetti.

5 ... ♗e7

As ♘g5 is now a very real threat, Black hastens to castle, 5 ... h6 (6 0-0 ♗e7) is likely to transpose into the note to Black's sixth move. The advantage is that many of White's wilder possibilities are hereby avoided; the drawback is that ... h6 might not be a particularly useful move.

6 0-0

The best move, but it is as well to know that various alternatives, which, though inferior, are nevertheless not without danger for Black.

a) 6 ♗xf7+? (the exchange on e5, considered below, is the necessary prelude to this sacrifice/combination) 6 ...♚xf7 7 ♘g5+ ♚g8! (7 ... ♚g6 might be playable as well, Shtadler - Perevorznik, Women's Candidates 1967, continued: 8 h4 h5 9 f4 ef 10 ♘e2 ♕g8 11 ♘xf4+ ♚h6 12 ♘d5 ♘xd5 13 ♘e6+ ♚g6 14 ed ♘f6 15 ♕d3+ ♚f7 when White was already losing, but the main line is so convincing that it seems pointless to bother with this. The moves 7 ... ♚e8 and 7 ... ♚f8 both lose the queen and are definitely to be avoided!) 8 ♘e6 ♕e8 9 ♘xc7 ♕g6 10 ♘xa8 (perhaps it is better to make a genuine sacrifice out of this by 10 0-0!? ♖b8 11 ♕d3 h6 12 f4 as in Brinckmann – Romin, Hamburg 1930, although objectively, White is lost. 10 de? ♘xe5 just brings the black pieces nearer the white king) 10 ... ♕xg2 11 ♖f1 ed (this is why it is better for White to exchange first on e5, the e5 square becomes accessible to the black knight) 12 ♕xd4 (this seems obvious, but *12 ♕e2* has also been played; *12 ... dc!* 12 ... ♘e5 is met by 13 f4. *13 ♕c4+ d5 14 ♕xc8+ ♔f7 15 ♕xb7.* Trying to keep the queen in the game; the greedy 15 ♕xh8 loses to 15 ... ♕xe4+ 16 ♔d1 ♕f3+ 17 ♔e1 cb 18 ♗xb2 ♗b4+ 19 c3 ♗xc3+ 20 ♗xc3 ♕xc3+ 21 ♔e2 ♕c2+ 22 ♔f3 – 22 ♔e1 ♘e5 threatening ... ♘d3 and ... ♘f3 mate, or 22 ♔f3 ♕e4+ 23 ♔g3 ♕g4 mate – 22 ... d4+ *(93)* fresh wood on the fire!

This is the most fun, although there may be other ways for Black to win, 23 ♔xd4 – 23 ♔f3 and 23 ♔f4 are both answered by 23 ... ♕e4+ and 24 ... ♕g4 mate – 23 ... ♕c5+ 24 ♔d3 ♘e5+ – Black's three pieces cooperate well, and all the

white pieces, stuck in the corners, are mere witnesses to the persecution of the white king 25 ♔d2 – or 25 ♔e2 ♕c2+ 26 ♔e3 ♕d3+ and mate in two moves – 25 ... ♘e4+ and, by my calculation, White is mated in at most five moves.

Alternatively, 16 ♗e3 cb 17 ♖b1 ♗b4+ 18 ♔d1 ♕f3 mate, or 18 c3 ♕xb1+, ... ♕xf1+ and ... b1(♕)+ with material advantage, finally 17 ♖d1 ♕xc2 menacing ... ♗b4+, ... b1(♕) or ... ♕xd1+ as appropriate. *15 ... ♕xe4+ 16 ♗e3 ♖b8 17 ♕xa7 cb 18 ♔d2.* Resigns might have been a better choice. *18 ... ♕b4+! 19 c3 ♘e4+ 20 ♔c2 ♘xc3+ 21 ♔f3 ♕e4+ 22 ♔g3 ♘e2+ 23 ♔h3 ♕f3 (94)* mate. Rabinovich – Ilyin-Zhenevsky, Moscow 1922) 12 ... ♘e5 13 f4 ♘fg4! 14 ♕d5+! (this forces the knight to retreat as 14 ... ♔f8?? allows 15 fe+!) 14 ... ♘f7 15 ♕c4 (defending f1 and threatening c8) 15 ... ♗h4+

16 ♔d1 ♗e6! 17 ♕e2 ♘f2+ 18 ♖xf2 (18 ♔d2 ♗g4 19 ♖xf2 ♗xf2 20 ♕b5 is best answered by 20 ... g6 – 21 ♕e8 mate was the threat – when White has hardly got a move, i.e: 21 ♘c7 ♗b6+) 18 ... ♗xf2 19 f5 (to stop 19 ... ♗g4) 19 ... ♕g1+ 20 ♔d2 (and now Black has a draw if he so wishes, by 20 ... ♕d5+, but instead he found a most beautiful win) 20 ... ♘e5!! *(95)*

21 ♘d1? (A blunder; this stops ... ♗e3+ but not ... ♗e1+. It would have been better to take the piece and see: 21 fe ♗e1+! 22 ♕xe1 ♘f3+ 23 ♔e2 ♘xe1 24 ♗e3 –

24 ♘d2 amounts to the same – 24 ... ♕xh2+ 25 ♔xe1 ♕h1+ 26 ♔e2 ♕xa1 – the queen's rooks don't seem to fare too well in this variation! – 27 ♘c7 h5! and the h-pawn will win, 28 e7 being answered by 28 ... ♔f7∓) 21 ... ♗e1+ 22 ♕xe1 ♕d4+ 23 ♔e2 ♗c4 mate! Heidenfeld – Wolpert, Johannesburg 1955.

b) **6 de** de (this is the normal move here, but *6 ... ♘xe5* is also very satisfactory, and may appeal to those players who don't wish to play the long, forcing main line. *7 ♗e2* is supposed to be a little better for White. Instead, 7 ♘xe5 de 8 ♕xd8+ ♗xd8 9 a4 – 9 ♗g5 0-0 10 0-0-0 is a recommendation of Alekhine's, but after 10 ... c6 11 a4 a6 the threat of ... b5-b4 allows Black to enjoy a certain amount of initiative on the queenside – 9 ... c6 10 a5 ♗e7 11 f3 ♘d7 12 ♘d1 ♘c5= Juhtman – Gusev, **USSR 1956**; 7 ♗b3? ♗g4 is ∓. Now *7 ... ♘xf3+* is the most logical, displacing the bishop but 7 ... ♘g6!? is also plausible. *8 ♗xf3 0-0 9 0-0 ♖e8*. 9 ... c6 was played in Birmingham – Manouck, French Ch 1986, which continued 10 a4 a5 11 ♕d4 ♗g4 12 ♗xg4 ♘xg4 13 ♗f4 ♕c7 14 ♖ad1 ♖ad8 with a quick draw, and Pickett likes the idea of playing, after 9 ... c6 10 ♗f4, 10 ... ♘e8!?, then ... f5, ... fe, and ... d5. My opinion is that 9 ... c6 is an unnecessary weakening of d6. *10 ♖e1 h6 11 b3* when Pachman - Dunkelblum, Dublin 1957, went on: *11 ... ♗f8?! 12 ♗b2 g6 13 ♘b5 ♗g7 14 c4* with a slight pull for White, but *ECO*'s recommendation, *11 ... ♘h7! 12 ♘d5 ♗f6 13 ♘xf6+ ♕xf6* is very strong, e.g: *14 ♗d2 ♘g5 15 ♗xg5 hg (96)∓* planning ... ♖e5, ... ♗d7-c6, ... ♖ae8

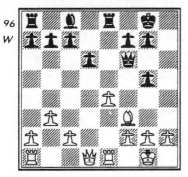

96
W

with powerful pressure on the white e-pawn) *7 ♗xf7+* (without this move there would be little point in White exchanging on e5, *7 ♕e2* is simply answered by *7 ... 0-0* followed by ... c6 when Black has a position that resembles various lines of the Pirc, with the difference that his king's bishop is more actively placed than on g7. There is another crude attempt by

White: *7 ♘g5?! 0-0 8 ♗xf7+ ♖xf7 9 ♘e6.* Obviously 9 ♘xf7 would already be better for Black, two pieces are worth more than a rook and a pawn in the middle game, other things being equal. In general I am very suspicious of lines like this that give away a piece to win the rook on a8, the knight on a8 never seems to come out again. *9 ... ♕e8 10 ♘xc7 ♕d8 11 ♘xa8.* 11 ♘e6? does not force a draw as now the black queen can escape to the b6 or a5 squares. *11 ... b5.* This is probably the strongest, although Larsen gives the following, pretty possibility: *11 ... ♗b4!? 12 ♗d2 b6 13 ♘b5?! ♗xd2+ 14 ♕xd2 ♘xe4 15 ♕d5 ♗b7!?* as 16 ♕xb7 ♘dc5 wins the white queen, although *17 ♖d1 ♕f6 18 ♕xf7+ ♔xf7 19 0-0 ♕c6* is not clear even though the white knights look a little silly. *12 ♘d5.* The idea is to rescue the knight on a8, 12 ♘xb5 is pointless: *12 ... ♕a5+ 13 ♘c3 ♘xe4 14 0-0 ♘xc3 15 bc ♕xc3 16 ♗e3 ♕c6 17 ♗xa7 ♗b7∓. 12 ... ♗d6!* Pickett suggests *12 ... ♘xe4 13 0-0 ♗d6 14 ♕d3 ♗b7* e.g: *15 ♕xe4 ♗xa8 16 ♖d1 ♘b6* but not *12 ... ♘xd5?! 13 ♕xd5 ♘f6 14 ♕xb5* and White went on to win Magerut - Freidin, USSR 1955. *13*

0-0. 13 ♗g5 ♗b7 14 ♕d2 ♗xa8 15 0-0-0 ♗f8 also worked out well for Black in Braminsky – Hever, USSR 1965. *13 ... ♗b7 14 ♘8c7 ♗xc7∓* Arulaid – Heuer, Tartu 1970. Providing that Black can avoid too many exchanges, and find some good sites for his minor pieces, things should go well) *7 ... ♔xf7 8 ♘g5+ ♔g8* (*8 ... ♔g6!* may well be even stronger, but it demands a certain amount of courage on the part of Black to play it: *9 h4.* The point is that after 9 ♘e6 ♕g8! 10 ♘xc7 ♖b8 saves the rook-+; 9 f4 ef 10 ♘e6 ♕g8 11 ♘xf4 ♘e5! – probably simpler than 11 ... ♖b8 12 ♗xf4 – 12 ♘xa8 ♗g4 13 ♘e2 ♕c4∓ – Harding, Black has an attack, and when he takes on a8, a material advantage to boot! *9 ... h5 10 f4 ef.* 10 ... ♘c5?! 11 f5+ ♗xf5 12 ef+ ♔xf5 is also possible, if not without risk! *11 ♘e2.* 11 ♘e6 is no improvement: 11 ... ♕g8 12 ♘xc7 ♘e5! 13 ♘xa8 ♗g4 14 ♕d4 ♘c6 15 ♕a4 ♕b8 16 ♕b5 f3! *(97)*
0-1 Rosen – Schoizswohl, European Cup final 1960/1, as .... ♕g3+ will be curtains; did White really sacrifice a piece to lose so ignominiously? *11 ... ♗d6 12 e5.* There is nothing to be had from 12 ♗xf4 ♘e5∓. *12 ... ♘xe5!*

97
W

13 ♘xf4+ ♔h6 14 ♘f7+ ♔xf7 15 ♘e6+ ♔h7 16 ♘xd8 ♖xd8 (98)

98
W

Analysis by Voronkov, when Black is winning; not only has he three pieces for the queen, but also two enticing squares for his pieces on g4 and g3, and, on top of this, the white king is stuck in the centre) 9 ♘e6 ♕e8 10 ♘xc7 ♕g6 11 ♘xa8 ♕xg2 12 ♖f1 ♘c5 13 ♔e2 ♗h3 14 ♗e3 ♕xf1+ 15 ♕xf1 ♗xf1 16 ♔xf1 ♔f7 (this is solid enough, but why not try to keep the a8 knight out of the game with 16 ... ♘e6!?, for example: 17 ♘d5 ♔f7 18 ♘ac7 ♘xc7 19 ♘xc7 ♖c8 20

Nd5 Rxc2 21 Nxe7 Kxe7 22 Bxa7 Rxb2∓/± or 17 Bxa7 Kf7 18 Nb6 Bc5 though there is a risk that 19 Nca4 might just be good for White) 17 Nc7 Nfxe4 18 Nxe4 Nxe4 19 Nd5 Bc5=. If Black wants to win then either 8 ... Kg6! or perhaps 6 ... Nxe5 are better.

c) **6 Ng5?!** This is similar to the above material: 6 ... 0-0 7 Bxf7+ Rxf7 8 Ne6 Qe8 9 Nxc7 Qd8 10 Nxa8 b5! (again, the key move – the idea is that although White has the material advantage – exchange and two pawns – sooner or later he will try to develop the rest of his pieces and castle. Black, therefore, wants to take the knight on a8, but at the same time he aims to create complications, provoke weaknesses or regain some pawns. This is the point of ... b5, Black prepares ... Bb7 x a8, but also has the b4 move if need be. Other moves are worse: 10 ... b6 11 de Nxe5 12 f4 Ng6 13 Be3 Bb7 14 Nxb6 ab 15 Qd4±, Henneberger – Sollerm, Zurich 1942; or 10 ... Qa5 11 0-0 b5 12 de Nxe5 13 Nd5±; or 10 ... ed 11 Qxd4 Ng4 12 0-0 b6 13 h3 N4e5 14 Nd5 – threat: Nac7 – 14 ... Ba6 15 Nxe7+ Rxe7 16 Rd1 Qxa8 17 Qxd6 Qxe4 18 Qd5+∞) 11 de (11 Nxb5 Qa5+ 12 Nc3 Nxe4 is very much to Black's taste: 13 0-0 Nxc3 14 bc Qxc3 15 Be3 Bb7 16 de Nxe5 17 Bxa7 Bxa8 – or even 17 ... Nf3+!? – and the black pieces are pointing very aggressively toward the white king, either ... Nf3+ or ... Bf3 may well be on the cards soon. Alternatively, 11 f3!? Bb7 12 Nxb5 and instead of 12 ... Bxa8 13 d5= Ericsson – Schonman, what about 12 ... Qa5+ 13 Nc3 d5!? opening up the position to good effect e.g: 14 0-0 ed 15 Qxd4?? Bc5-+) 11 ... Nxe5 (of course, 11 ... de transposes to note 'b' and can't be bad, but it seems more natural to put the queen's knight on a more advanced square) 12 Bf4 (A good move; 12 Nxb5 Qa5+ 13 Nc3 Nxe4 gives Black all the chances, whilst 12 0-0 is risky, the white king being safer on the queenside: 12 ... Bb7 13 f3 b4 14 Nd5 Nxd5 – or 14 ... Bxd5 – 15 ed Qxa8 is already ∓, and 12 f4 is well answered by 12 ... Nc4 whilst 12 Nd5 Nxd5 13 Qxd5 Qd7 is ∓ according to Keres) 12 ... Ng6! (12 ... b4 occurred in Murey – Ree Suhumi 1972, 13 Nd5 Nxd5 14 Qxd5 Ng6 15 Bg3 Bf8 16 0-0-0 Bb7 17 Qe6 Qxa8 18 f3± but 18 ... Bc8 19 Qc4 Ne5?? 20 Bxe5 de 21 Rd8

♗e6 22 ♖xf8+ 1-0 and 12 ...
♗b7? 13 ♕d4! ♗xa8 14 0-0-0
♘fd7 15 ♗xe5 de 16 ♕xa7 is
±. The following is my analysis, and there is no
guarantee!) 13 ♗g3 ♗b7 14
♕d4 ♕xa8! (removing the
queen from the d-file and
putting more pressure on
the e-pawn). Now there are
several possibilities:

c1) **15 0-0-0** ♘xe4 16
♘xe4 ♗xe4 17 ♗xd6? ♕c6!
(99) winning,

due to 18 c3 ♗g5+, or 18 ♕c3
♗xd6 19 ♕xc6 ♗f4+, or 18
♖d2 ♗g5. Or alternatively
17 f3 ♗f5 18 ♗xd6 ♗f6 19
♕d2 ♕c8 20 g4? ♗g5∓ or 19
♕d5 ♕c8 20 ♕c5 ♕xc5 21
♗xc5 ♖c7 22 b4 ♘f4 giving
Black plenty of play around
the weakened white queen-
side.

c2) **15 f3** b4!? 16 ♘e2 (16
♕xb4? d5 and Black's
pieces come alive) 16 ... ♗a6
(keeping the king in the
centre) 17 ♗xd6? ♗xd6 18
♕xd6 ♗xe2 19 ♔xe2 ♘xe4
20 fe ♕xe4+ with a strong

attack for the exchange.

c3) **15 ♗xd6** ♘xe4 16
♘xe4 ♗xe4 17 ♗xe7 (17
0-0-0? ♕c6! has been seen
before!) 17 ... ♖xe7 18 0-0-0
♗xg2 with advantage to
Black, even the endings are
very favourable for him
now.

d) Finally, moves like
6 h3 will transpose into the
next chapter after 6 ... 0-0
7 0-0. Likewise **6 a4** 0-0
when 7 0-0 is best, for if
White leaves his king in the
centre too long Black can
strike out dangerously: 7
a5?! ed 8 ♘xd4 (8 ♕xd4
♘g4, ... ♗f6 etc) 8 ... ♘c5 9
♕e2 ♖e8 10 0-0 ♗f8 11 ♗g5
(11 f3? d5 12 ♘xd5? ♘xd5 13
♗xd5 c6∓) 11 ... ♘e6 with
reasonable play.

6 ...   0-0

This is the normal, and
the best move here, but
Black can also try to develop his queenside play
whilst delaying castling
(variations below) or he can
forget castling altogether,
leave his king in the middle
and attack on the kingside
by way of ... h6, ... g5 ...
♘f8-g6-f4; although this
can prove dangerous ag-
ainst an unprepared oppo-
nent, it is objectively in-
correct (variation b).

a) **6 ... c6** 7 a4 (it is best
to stop Black playing ... b5)
7 ... ♕c7 (alternatively, 7 ...

b6 8 ♕e2 a6?, when Black is ready to play ... ♗b7 and ... b5 with good play on the queenside. Unfortunately: *9 ♖d1 ♕c7 (100)*

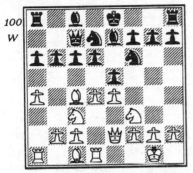

10 ♗xf7+ ♔xf7 11 ♘g5+ ♔g6. 11 ... ♔g8 is now met by 12 ♕c4++-. *12 ♖d3 ♕b7,* Christiansen – Andonov, Saint John 1988, when, instead of 13 ♖g3 with a strong attack, *13 de ♘xe5 14 f4! ♘xd3 15 f5+ ♗xf5 16 ef+ ♔xf5 17 ♕xd3+ ♔e5 18 ♗f4+ ♔xf4 19 ♘e6+ ♔e5 20 ♖e1+ ♘e4 21 ♕xe4+ ♔f6 22 ♖f1* was mate) 8 ♕e2 ♘b6? (8 ... 0-0) 9 de de 10 ♗xf7+! ♔xf7 11 a5 ♘bd7 12 ♕c4+ ♔e8 (12 ... ♔g6 13 ♘h4+ ♔h5 14 ♕e2+ ♔xh4 15 g3+ ♔h3 16 f3+-) 13 ♘g5 ♘f8 14 ♖d1 ♗d7 15 ♗e3! ♕c8 16 ♕f7+ ♔d8 17 ♘a4 c5 18 ♘xc5! ♗xc5 19 ♕xg7+- ♘g6 20 ♗xc5 ♘h5 21 ♗e7+ ♔c7 22 ♗d6+ ♔c6 23 ♕f7 ♔b5 24 a6! ba *(101)* Velimirovic – Kavalek, Belgrade 1965, and now the easiest way to win was: 25 ♕b3+! ♔c6 26

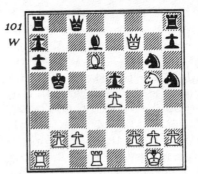

♖xa6+! ♕xa6 27 ♕d5+ with mate in two.

b) **6 ... h6** 7 a4 (this is still a useful move, *7 ♗e3 c6 8 ♗b3?!* Or 8 de de 9 ♕e2 b5 10 ♗b3 ♕c7 reaching a game Thomas – Alekhine, Hastings 1934, which Alekhine handled in a slightly different manner: 11 a3 ♘c5 12 ♗a2 ♘e6! 13 ♖fd1 ♗g4 14 ♘e1 ♘d4 15 ♕d2 0-0 - only now - 16 h3 ♘xe3 17 ♕xe3 a5 18 ♘e2 ♗c5 with a small advantage for Black. *8 ... ♕c7 9 ♘d2 g5!? 10 a4 ♘f8 11 a5 ♘g6 12 ♖e1 ♘f4 13 f3 ♖g8 14 ♖f1 ♗e6 15 ♘g3 ♕d7 16 d5 ♗h3! 17 gh ♕xh3 18 ♕d2 ♘6h5 19 ♕f2 g4 20 ♔h1 gf 21 ♖g1 ♗h4 22 ♗xf4 ef 23 ♘xh5 ♗xf2* and went on to win, Yates – Marco, The Hague 1921) 7 ... c6 8 b3 (This might be the best, but the alternatives are interesting too: *8 h3 ♕c7 9 ♗e3.* Or 9 ♖e1 g5 10 ♘h2 ♘f8 11 ♘f1 ♘e6 12 de de 13 ♘g3 ♘f4∞ Ciric – Ree, Beverwijk 1967. *9 ... g5!?* Or first

9 ... ♘f8!? 10 ♘h2 g5 11 ♘g4?! - I prefer 11 ♘f1 as above - 11 ... ♗xg4 12 hg ♘g6 13 g3 h5 with wild play; Zatulovskaya - Dmitrieva, USSR 1963. *10 ♖e1.* Not 10 de de 11 ♘d2? ♘f8 12 ♘e2 ♘g6 13 c3 ♘f4 14 b4 h5 15 ♕b3 ♖h7 16 ♖fe1 ♖g7 - storm clouds are gathering - 17 a5 h4 18 ♗xf4 gf 19 ♔h2 ♕d7 - threat: ... ♖xg2+ - 20 ♔h1 ♔f8! - since 20 ... ♖xg2? 21 ♗xf7+ ♔f8 22 ♗e6 - 21 ♖ad1 ♖xg2! *(102)*

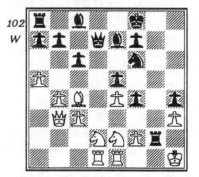

22 ♗e6 ♕d3! 23 ♗xc8 ♖xf2! 24 ♕c4 ♕e3 - menacing ... f3 and ... ♖xh2+ - 25 ♖f1 ♖xe2 0-1, Jamieson - Rogers. This is the sort of planless play that White must avoid if he doesn't want to get crushed. *10 ... ♘f8?* This loses. Jurtajev suggests first 10 ... ♖g8 as unclear. At the moment the black rook is unfortunately placed on h8. *11 de de (103) 12 ♘xe5! ♕xe5 13 ♗d4 ♕a5 14 e5 ♘d5 15 e6 f6 16 ♘xd5 cd 17 ♗b5+ ♔d8 18 ♗c3 ♕b6*

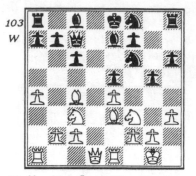

19 ♕xd5+ ♔c7 20 a5! winning easily, Jurtajev - Palatnik, Frunze 1979: alternatively *8 ♕e2 g5!?* 8 ... ♕c7 is more circumspect, but 9 ♖d1 ♘f8 10 ♘h4 g6 11 f4 ♗g4 12 ♘f3 ed 13 e5! was still ± in Ivanovic - Gliksman, Yugoslavia Ch 1968. *9 ♖d1 ♕c7 10 ♗e3 ♘f8 11 de de 12 ♘xe5!?* This is the same idea as above, but not so convincing. *12 ... ♕xe5 13 ♗d4 ♕f4! 14 g3!? ♕g4 15 f3 ♕h5?! 16 e5 ♘g8 17 g4 ♕g6 18 e6 ♖h7 19 ef+ ♖xf7 20 ♖e1 ♗d7 21 ♖ad1 0-0-0 22 ♗xf7 ♕xf7 23 ♗xa7±* Peters - Shipman, Las Vegas 1976) 8 ... ♕c7 9 ♗b2 ♘f8?! (White is well placed to refute this, but nevertheless, 9 ... 0-0 would have been somewhat to White's advantage anyway as a later ♘h4 would threaten not only ♘f5, but also ♘g6, as Black has weakened g6) 10 de de 11 ♘xe5! (again!) 11 ... ♕xe5 *(104)* 12 ♘d5! (the point; 12 ...

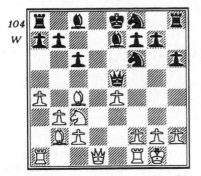

104
W

♛xb2?? allows 13 ♘c7 mate) 12 ... ♛d6 13 ♗a3 cd (or 13 ... c5 14 e5 ♛xe5 15 ♖e1 ♘e4 16 ♖xe4 ♛xe4 17 ♘c7 mate) 14 ♗xd6 dc 15 ♗xe7 ♚xe7 16 e5 ♘fd7 17 ♛d6+± Nimzowitsch - Marco, Gothenburg 1920. The black position is completely disorganised.

This furnishes ample proof that 6 ... 0-0 is indisputably Black's best move at this juncture. We have now reached the main starting position for the Hanham, and White's various seventh moves, and Black's appropriate strategems, will be discussed in the next chapter.

9) Hanham Variation – Main Line

1	e4	e5
2	♘f3	d6
3	d4	♘f6
4	♘c3	♘bd7
5	♗c4	♗e7
6	0-0	0-0 *(105)*

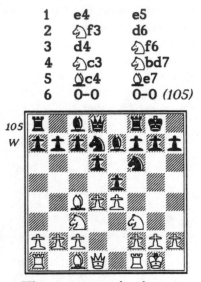

Thus we reach the starting point for the main line. White has a big choice of moves here, but only two, variations B and C, really address themselves to the problems facing White. Happily for Black, variation A, which was long considered to be White's best, now seems to be a mistake.

With accurate play White can maintain an edge, but in the ensuing manoeuvring it is often the player who knows what he is doing

who will come out on top.

Black normally tries to gain room on the queenside but should be ready to capture on d4 and pressurize e4 when appropriate.

White's alternatives are arranged as follows:

A 7 ♕e2?!
B 7 ♖e1
C 7 a4 (without ♖e1)
D Others

A

7   ♕e2?!

And Black's main two replies are further subdivided:

A1 7 ... ed!
A2 7 ... c6

A1

7	...	ed!
8	♘xd4	♘e5!

The most aggressive, and the start of an interesting sequence of moves that seek to exploit the fact that the white queen occupies the best retreat square of both bishop and knight. **8 ... ♘b6?!** is worse, as the knight is almost always misplaced on this square, the game Gufeld - Lerner, USSR 1978, continuing: 9 ♗b3 c5 10 ♘f3 ♗g4 11 a4 ♛c7 12 ♗f4 c4 13 ♗a2 ♖fc8 14 h3 ♗xf3 15 ♛xf3 ♛c6 16 a5 ♘bd7 and although Black has managed to shut the White king's bishop out of the game, he has had to make too many positional concessions and White is better. **8 ... ♖e8??** is a blunder here, which was neatly refuted in Tylor - Koltanowski, Hastings 1931: 9 ♗xf7+! ♔xf7 10 ♘e6! ♔xe6 11 ♛c4+ d5 12 ed+ ♔f7 13 d6+ and dc, winning Black's trapped queen. If Black wishes to play like this then 8 ... ♘c5 first, then ... ♖e8 and ... ♗f8 is possible, compare with A21.

9   ♗b3

If White does not move this bishop, then he can forget about an opening advantage, and he might even be worse in the long term because of Black's bishop pair. One example: 9 f4? ♘xc4 10 ♛xc4 ♘xe4! 11 ♘xe4 d5 12 ♛d3 de 13 ♛xe4 ♗c5∓. And 9 ♗b5? a6 10 f4 (10 ♗a4? c5 and ... b5∓) 10 ... ♗g4 11 ♛f2 ab 12 fe de 13 ♘dxb5 c6∓ is just plain bad.

9   ...   c5!

10   ♘f5

Of course, this knight would like to go to e2 and then to f4 to control d5, which Black has just weakened, but the white queen is already there. The alternatives are not particularly enticing either: **10 ♘bd5?** a6 11 ♘a3 b5 12 ♗d5 (12 f4?! ♘g6 13 ♗d5 ♖a7 15 ♘ab1 b4 15 ♘d1 ♘xd5∓) 12 ... ♖a7 13 ♘d1 ♘xd5 14 ed ♗f6∓ or **10 ♘f3?** ♗g4 11 ♗f4 ♗xf3! 12 gf ♘g6 13 ♗g3 (not 13 ♛d2? ♛c8 - menacing ... c4, ... a6, and ... b5, ensnaring the bishop - 14 ♗d5 ♘h4 15 ♛e3?! - White is lost anyway - 15 ... ♛h3 and mate next go) 13 ... ♘h5 14 ♘d5 ♗g5∓, Black can play for ... ♔h8 and ... f5, or for control of the kingside dark squares, i.e: 15 ♖ad1 ♘hf4 16 ♘xf4 ♗xf4 17 ♗d5 ♛f6 18 c3 h5-h4 etc.

10   ...   ♗xf5

11   ef   ♛d7! *(106)*

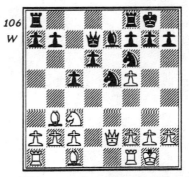

This is the point, Black has an extra centre pawn and can pressure White's forward f-pawn, gaining time for development. Formerly 11 ... ♖c8 had been played but this is not a useful move: 12 ♘d5 ♕d7 13 f4 ♘c6 14 g4 ♘d4 15 ♕d1! b5 16 ♗g2 b4 17 ♘e2 ♘xe2+ 18 ♕xe2 d5 19 ♖d1±, Boleslavsky - Furman, Moscow 1961. However 11 ... ♖e8 is playable, similar to A21.

12 ♗f4

This seems best. 12 ♘d5 ♖fe8 13 ♖d1! (struggling for control of d5; 13 c3 ♗d8 14 ♘xf6+ ♗xf6 15 ♘d5 ♕xf5 16 ♗xb7 ♖ad8∓, compare with Ahman - Brglez, in A21) 13 ... ♗d8 14 ♘e3 ♘c6? (14 ... ♗c7 first looks better: 15 c3 ♖e7 when it is difficult to see a move for White e.g: 16 f4? ♘eg4 or 16 ♗d2 d5) 15 c3 ♗c7 16 ♕f3 ♖e5 17 g4 ♖ae8 18 g5 ♘e4 19 h4 ♘e7! 20 ♘g4 ♘xf5 21 ♘xe5 ♖xe5 22 ♕g4 c4 23 ♗c2 (else 23 ... ♗b6) *(107)*

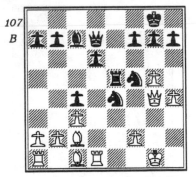

23 ... ♘xf2! 24 ♔xf2 ♗b6+ and now, instead of 25 ♖d4? g6 26 ♗f4 ♕b5! winn-

ing, Palciauskas - Staal, Corr 1975; 25 ♔f3! ♕c6+ 26 ♗e4 ♖xe4 27 ♕xe4 ♘xh4+ 28 ♔f4 ♘g2+ is a draw by perpetual check.

12 f4!? ♘c6 13 g4 has been mooted, but I think that 13 ... d5! 14 g5 (this is better than *14 ♕g2 c4 15 ♗a4 ♖fe8?! 15 ... ♗c5+ 16 ♔h1 ♖fe8 is crushing, if 17 g5 ♘e4∓. 16 ♗e3 ♗a3! 17 ♗d4 ♗xb2 18 ♖ad1! I had originally thought that White would try 18 ♗xf6?! gf 19 ♘xd5 but then 19 ... ♗d4+! 20 ♔h1 ♖ad8 21 ♘b4 ♗xa1 22 ♖xa1 ♕d1+ wins the house. 18 ... ♗xc3 19 ♗xc3 ♘e4 20 ♗e5! ♕d8*. Else 21 ♕xe4; now White had to try 21 ♗xc6 bc 22 g5 f6∓, but *21 g5? b5! 22 ♗xb5 ♕b6+ 23 ♔h1 ♕xb5 24 ♗xg7 ♔xg7 25 ♕h3*. White has no real compensation for the two horses. *25 ... ♔h8 26 f6 d4 27 ♖f3 ♕d5 28 ♕g2 ♕f5 29 ♖h3 ♕xh3* 0-1, Fabiano - Kosten, San Bennedetto 1991. The best reply to *14 ♖d1 is probably 14 ... ♘d4 15 ♕g2 c4!? 16 ♖xd4 ♗c5 17 ♗e3 cb. Or first ... ♗xd4. 18 ab ♖e8*, when it is unlikely that White has enough compensation for the exchange) 14 ... c4 15 gf (15 ♗a4 ♖fe8 16 ♕g2 - not 16 gf?? ♗c5+ - 16 ... ♗c5+ 17 ♔h1 ♘e4∓) 15 ... ♗xf6 16 ♗a4 ♕xf5 is a very promising piece sacrifice: 17 ♗xc6 bc 18 ♖e1!? ♖ae8! 19 ♕xe8 ♕g4+ is at least a draw, e.g: 20 ♔f2 ♗d4+ 21 ♕e3 ♕xf4+−+, or 18 ♗d2 ♕xc2 (simplest, but 18 ... ♖fe8 19 ♕d1 d4 20 ♘e2 c3! has its points) with three pawns and a harmonious position for the piece *(108)*.

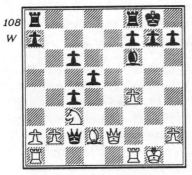

108
W

I certainly wouldn't want to get this position with White!

12	...	♘c6
13	♘d5	♖ae8
14	c3	♕xf5
15	♕d2	♘xd5
16	♗xd5	♘d4!?
17	♗c4	

The only move against the threats of ... ♕xd5 and ... ♕xf4 and ... ♘e2+. 17 cd? ♕xd5 leaves White a pawn down for nothing.

17	...	♘e6
18	♗g3	♖d8
19	♖ad1	

Unfortunately, Black now spoiled his preceding play with 19 ... ♔h8? 20 ♖fe1 g6?±, although White also

went astray and Black won anyway, Pfannkuche – S Bucker, Sudlohn 1986. Of course, Black should be trying to advance his extra (backward) pawn; the correct move is therefore 19 ... ♘c7! controlling d5, 20 ♖fe1 (20 a4?! ♗g5 21 f4 ♗f6 and ... d5) 20 ... ♕d7 21 ♗d5 ♘xd5 22 ♕xd5 ♖fe8 23 c4 (attempting to keep the pawn from advancing) 23 ... ♗f8 followed by ... ♖e6 etc. White has some drawing chances, but if I had a position like this every time I had Black, then I would be a very happy man!

A2

7	...	c6
8	a4	

Ostensibly Black was threatening ... b5 so White immediately clamps down on b5. The alternatives are nothing for White: **8 ♗b3** b5! 9 d5? (9 a3 a6 is more sensible, but this is exactly the sort of queenside structure that Black is after) 9 ... b4 10 dc bc 11 cd ♗b7! 12 bc ♘xe4 13 ♕d3 ♘c5 14 ♕e3 ♕xd7 *(109)*∓, Graf – Harding, London 1973; the position resembles a Sicilian where Black has sacrificed the exchange on c3, except that Black isn't an exchange down!

8 ♖d1 b5! (*8 ... ♕a5?* is

not a move Black often plays in Hanham's, and in the game Campora – Costa, Bern 1987, we got an idea why: *9 a4 b5? 10 b4! ♛xb4 11 ab ♘b6.* 11 ... ♛xc3 12 ♗d2 ♛xc2 13 ♖fc1 ♛b2 14 ♖cb1 ♛c2 15 ♗d3± but the queen manages to get itself lost anyhow. *12 ♗d3 ed 13 ♘b1 c5 14 ♗d2 ♛b2 15 ♘a3 ♘a4 16 ♘c4 ♘c3 17 ♗xc3 1-0.* Of course *17 ♘xb2 ♘xe2+ 18 ♗xe2* wasn't bad, but *17 ♗xc3 ♛xc3 18 ♖fb1* and ♘a3 is stronger) 9 de de 10 ♗b3 ♛c7 11 a4 b4 12 ♘b1 ♘c5∓. 8 ♗g5?! h6 transposes to Dd, and 8 de?! ♘xe5 9 ♘xe5 de is most satisfactory for Black.

Now there is another parting of the ways:

A21 8 ... ed!
A22 8 ... ♛c7 and others

In the first variation, Black opens the game up and play will be similar to A1, and in the second, in general, he will keep the position closed.

A21

8 ... ed!
9 ♘xd4 ♘e5

This is, I believe, the best but Black has another interesting possibility in 9 ... **♖e8**, as 10 ♗xf7+ does not work anymore since the d5 square is guarded. So: 10 ♗a2 (*10 ♗e3 ♗f8 11 ♘f3.* Ready to answer 11 ... ♘xe4? with 12 ♘xe4 ♖xe4 13 ♗xf7+ ♔xf7 15 ♘g5+. *11 ... ♘e5 12 ♘xe5 de=*) 10 ... ♗f8 11 ♛f3 (the queen must get off the e-file) 11 ... ♘e5 (11 ... g6 and ♗g7 is worth trying) 12 ♛d1 (better than 12 ♛g3?! ♘h5 13 ♛g5 ♛xg5 14 ♗xg5 h6 15 ♗c1 ♘f6=, Marjanovic. Campora, Bor 1985) 12 ... ♘g6 (this is much more logical than *12 ... ♘fd7?*, which takes the pressure off e4, Gheorghiu – Panno, Manila 1976, continued: *13 f4 ♘g6 14 ♘f3 ♗e7 15 ♔h1 ♛c7 16 ♗e3.* Black has conceded the centre for nothing, things now go from bad to worse. *16 ... b6 17 ♛e2 ♗f6 18 ♘g5! ♘h8.* Unfortunately, 18 ... ♗xg5? fails to 19 ♗xf7+. *19 ♛h5 ♘f8 20 e5!±*) 13 ♖e1 (*13 ♘f3!?* is interesting) 13 ... a5 15 h3 h6 15 f4 ♗d7 16 ♔h1 c5 17 ♘f3 ♗c6 18 f5 ♘e5 19 ♗f4 ♛b6 20 ♗xe5! de 21

♕e2± Ivanovic - Najdorf, Bugojno 1982. White's possession of c4, d5 and b5 give him the edge, although he later lost (victim of Black's dark-squared bishop!).

9 ... ♘xe4? has some cute tactical points, but almost certainly loses: 10 ♘xe4! (this is far from obvious, the more natural *10 ♕xe4?* is worse: *10 ... d5 11 ♗xd5*. 11 ♘xd5?? cd 12 ♕xd5 ♘b6 0-1 Zeirbulis - Randviir, Parnu 1950; 12 ♗xd5 ♘f6 amounts to the same. *11 ... ♘f6 12 ♗xf7+ ♖xf7 13 ♕d3 ♘g4!* offers good play to Black e.g: *14 ♗e3?* 14 h3 ♘e5 15 ♕e4 is more circumspect. *14 ... ♕c7 15 g3 ♕e5 16 ♕e4 ♕h5 17 ♕h1 ♗c5!* with a dangerous initiative, Uhlin - Henningsen, West Germany 1966) 10 ... d5 11 ♘f5! (although 11 ♗a2 is also better for White: 11 ... de 12 ♖d1 ♗f6 13 ♘f5 ♕c7 4 ♕xe4, Suetin - Gusev, Tula 1950) 11 ... de (the first game with 11 ♘f5 continued: 11 ... dc? 12 ♗h6! ♘f6 13 ♘eg3 ♗xf5 14 ♘xf5 gh 15 ♘xe7++-, Tseshkovsky - Lutikov, Alma Ata 1968/9) 12 ♕xe4 ♗f6 13 ♖d1 (13 ♘h6+!? is fun: 13 ... gh 14 ♗d3 ♖e8 15 ♕xh7+ ♔f8 16 ♗xh6+ ♔e7 17 ♖fe1+ ♔d6 *(110)*

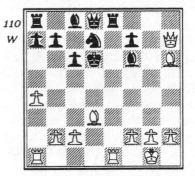

when 18 ♕xf7 would have kept the black king's chances of survival in doubt; as it was, in Gruzman - Pankravtov, USSR 1969, White got a bit carried away with his piece sacrifices and soon lost). After 13 ♖d1 the black position is probably lost, e.g: 13 ... ♕a5 (13 ... ♖e8 14 ♗xf7+ ♔xf7 15 ♘d6+ ♔f8 16 ♕xh7+-) 14 ♘e7+ ♗xe7 15 ♕xe7 ♘f6 16 ♗d2±.

10 ♗a2

This looks better than 10 ♗b3, though this has also been played, when Black can still play in similar style to 9 ... ♖e8 by playing:

a) **10 ... ♖e8!?** and it is interesting to watch the course of events in Howell - Barua, London 1990, 11 ♔h1?! (this is not very useful at the moment, perhaps 11 ♕d1!? - taking the queen from the e-file and leaving the e2 square for the knight should Black play ... c5 - 11 ... ♗f8 12 ♖e1 is best, similar to Ivanovic - Najdorf above) 11 ... ♗f8 12 ♗e3 c5! 13 ♘bd5 a6 14 ♘a3 ♘eg4! (it is amazing how powerful the Black initiative becomes after just one inaccurate move on White's part) 15 ♗g5 h6 16 ♗h4 g5! 17 ♗g3 d5 18 f3 c4! (Black is happy to give up a piece just to shut White's king's bishop out of the game; when it manages to return, it is already too late) 19 ♗a2 d4 20 ♘d1 ♗xa3 21 ba b5! 22 e5 ♘xe5 23 ♗xe5 ♕d5 24 ♖e1 ♘d7 25 f4 ♗b7 26 ♘b2 ♘xe5 27 fe ♖xe5 28 ♕f1 ♖ae8 *(111)*

111
W

29 ♖xe5 ♖xe5 (Black is operating with a 3:1 ratio in his favour on the kingside, whilst the bulk of White's forces are jammed on the a- and b-files) 30 ab ab 31 a4 ♕e4 32 ♗xc4 (desperation) 32 ... bc 33 ♘xc4 ♖f5 34 ♕g1 ♕c6 35 ♘a3 ♕c3 36 ♘b5 ♗xg2+ 0-1.

b) **10 ... c5!** (the position is almost identical to that in A1 - the difference being that the white a-pawn is on a4 instead of a2 - and play will, of course, be roughly equivalent. I prefer the move order in A1 as it gives White fewer options, particularly over the placement of his king's bishop. but this sequence of moves does have an individual significance as it can also arise from 7 a4 c6 8 ♕e2?! ed, etc) 11 ♘f5 ♗xf5 12 ef ♕d7 13 ♘d5 ♖fe8 14 c3 (this should be compared to the note to move twelve of A1, where ♖d1 was played) 14 ... ♗d8 15 ♘xf6+ ♗xf6 16 ♗d5 ♕xf5! 17 ♗xb7 ♖ad8 18 ♗e4 ♕e6 19 ♕c2 g6 20 ♗f4 d5 21 ♗xe5 (the advent of opposite coloured bishops does nothing to help White; he is just too far behind in development, and loses quickly) 21 ... ♗xe5 22 ♗f3 ♕f6 23 ♕d1 d4! *(112)*

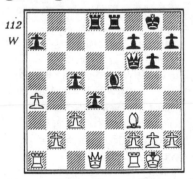

112
W

24 c4 d3 25 ♖a3 ♕f4 26 g3 ♕xc4 0-1, Ahman - Brglez, Corr 1982.

10	...	c5!
11	♘f5	

Unlike in A1, both 11 ♘db5 a6 12 ♘a3 and 11 ♘b3 ♗e6 12 ♘d2 are now playable, although Black is well placed in both cases.

11	...	♗xf5
12	ef	♖e8!

Essentially, this is the same as, or at least very similar to, variation A1. However, as the white bishop is now on a2 instead of b3, 10 ... ♕d7 is less strong because after 11 f4 ♘c6 12 g4 White is better, as Black's ... c4 no longer gains a tempo. Therefore, Black plays 12 ... ♖e8! and is ready to reply to 13 ♘d5 with ... ♕d7∓ as we have seen, whilst at the same time being well prepared for 13 f4 etc.

13	f4	♘c6
14	g4	d5!
15	♕g2!	

15 g5 reveals the point behind 12 ... ♖e8: 15 ... c4! (answering 16 gf?? with 16 ... ♗c5+ ♔h1 ♖xe2) 16 ♕d1 (else 16 ♕g2? ♗c5+ 17 ♔h1 ♘e4∓, or 16 ♕f2 ♘g4 17 ♕f3 ♗c5+ 18 ♔h1 ♘f2+ 19 ♖xf2 ♗xf2 20 ♕xf2 d4 21 ♘b5 a6 22 ♘a3 ♕d5+ 23 ♔g1 b5∓ as most of White's forces are 'sleeping') 16 ... ♗c5+ 17 ♔h1 (17 ♔g2 d4 18 ♘b5 ♕d5+ 19 ♕f3 ♖e2+ 20 ♖f2 ♖xf2+ 21 ♔xf2 d3+ 22 ♔g2 d2 23 ♕xd5 dc(♕)! should win, or 20 ♔h1 ♕xf3+ 21 ♖xf3 ♘g4∓) 17 ... d4 18 gf (18 ♘b5 a6 19 gf ab 20 ab ♘b4 or 19 ♘a3 ♕d5+ 20 ♕f3 ♖e1!

21 ♕xd5 ♖xf1+ 22 ♔g2 ♘xd5 23 ♔xf1 ♗xa3 24 ba b5∓) 18 ... dc 19 ♕xd8 ♖axd8 20 ♗xc4 ♘d4∓.

15	...	c4
16	♖d1	♕b6+
17	♔f1	♗b4!

Brglez's own improvement over another of his games: 17 ... d4 18 ♘e2 d3 19 cd cd 20 ♘c3 ♗b4 21 g5 ♗xc3 22 bc ♖e2 23 ♕g1 ♘g4 24 ♕xb6 ♘xh2+. Understandably, Black doesn't fancy playing the endgame with two knights against two bishops, so he decides to take the perpetual check: 25 ♔g1 ♘f3+ 26 ♔f1 ♘h2+ etc, ½-½ Keller - Brglez. Corr 1983.

18	g5	♗xc3
19	bc	♘e4
20	♖xd5	♘xc3
21	g6	

21 ♖d2? ♘xa2 22 ♖xa2 ♕b1∓ White wants to give up an exchange to free his bishop, but Black has other ideas!

21	...	♘xa2!
22	gf+	♔xf7
23	♖d7+	♖e7
24	♕d5+	♔e8
25	f6	(113)

A valiant try, 25 ... ♖xd7?? 26 ♕g8+ mate! However, it's difficult to believe anyone would fall for this in a correspondence game!

25	...	♘ab4!
26	♖xe7+	♘xe7

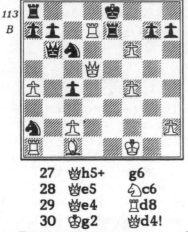

113
B

27	♕h5+	g6
28	♕e5	♘c6
29	♕e4	♖d8
30	♔g2	♕d4!

Forcing a winning endgame. The rest of the game requires no special comment: 31 ♕xd4 ♘xd4 32 fe ♖d7 33 ♖a2 ♖xe7 34 c3 ♘b3 35 ♗a3 ♖e3 36 ♗b4 a5 37 ♔f2 ♖h3 38 ♖e2+ ♔d8 39 ♔g2 ♖d3 40 ♗e7+ ♔d7 41 ♖e4 ♖xc3 42 ♗f6 ♖c2+ 43 ♔g3 ♘c5 44 ♖e7+ ♔d6 45 h4 ♘d7 46 ♖f7 ♘xf6 47 ♖xf6+ ♔e7 0-1, Povah – Brglez, Corr 1983.

It is important to study this line in conjunction with A1. My feeling is that they will eventually spell the end for 7 ♕e2. Still, there are a lot of points to be won for Black in the meantime whilst it is still White's most popular line.

A22

| | 8 | ... | ♕c7 |
| **and others** |

This is the pure Hanham continuation; Black tucks his queen away on c7, and lends extra support to his e-pawn. The black position is fairly robust, as always in this line, but a little worse.

| | 8 | ... | ♕c7 |

Apart from this and 8 ... ed!, **8 ... a5** is also a move of some interest, when Black's plan is to stop White expanding on the queenside. The drawback is that Black also deprives himself of any meaningful play in this sector, both ... b5 and ... c5 becoming impossible because of the weaknesses created on d5 and b5. It is very much a case, therefore, of Black adopting a 'wait and see' policy: (8 ... a5) 9 h3 (necessary to complete development with ♗e3, although it is possible to defer this; 9 ♖d1 ♕c7?! 10 h3 h6? 11 de de 12 ♘h4 ♘c5 13 ♘f5±, Kavalek – Najdorf, Manila 1973) 9 ... ♕e8!? (this is the start of Pickett's line, which formed the subject of his pamphlet. His idea is to put the queen on e7 where it helps defend f7, and to bring the king's bishop to the more active g1-a7 or h2-b8 diagonals. Although it does cost time, this manoeuvre is playable, and it is surprising that it hasn't proved more popular. Alternatively, 9 ... ♕c7?! 10 ♗a2! - better than putting this bishop on b3, as this encourages Black to play a later ... ed and ... ♘c5 - 10 ... h6?! 11 ♗e3 ♖e8? 12 ♕c4! ♗f8 13 ♖fd1 b6 14 de de 15 ♘b5 ♕b7 16 ♘d6 ♗xd6 17 ♖xd6 c5 18 ♖ad1 ♖a7 19 ♘d2 ♘e8 20 ♖d3 ♕c6 21 ♕b5 ♕g6 22 ♘c4 ♗a6 23 ♕b3±, Smejkal - Rukavina, Leningrad 1973. Or 9 ... ed?! - there is no justification for playing this now - 10 ♘xd4 ♘c5 11 ♖d1 ♕c7 12 ♗f4 ♘fd7 13 ♗g3 ♘e5 14 ♗a2 ♕b6 15 ♕e3 ♖e8 16 f4 ♘g6 17 ♗f2 ♕c7 18 ♕f3±, Smyslov - Lutikov, USSR 1959) 10 ♗e3 ♗d8 11 ♖ad1 ♕e7 12 ♗a2 (12 d5?! ♗b6 13 ♗xb6 ♘xb6 14 ♗b3 ♘h5 15 ♕d2 c5∓ - Pickett or 12 ♖fe1 ♗b6 13 de de 14 ♗xb6 ♘xb6 15 ♗a2 ♗e6 16 ♗xe6 ♕xe6 nearly =. It is worth noting a trap spotted by Harding in a similar position: 17 ♕e3?! ♘c4 18 ♕c5?? b6 winning) 12 ... ♗c7 *(114)* with reasonable chances.

It is a mistake to play **8 ... h6?!** however, after all didn't we all learn when we started playing chess not to move the pawns in front of our king without reason? 9 ♗a2! (although 9 ♗b3 ♕c7 10 h3 ♔h7 11 ♗e3 g6 12 ♖ad1 ♔g7 13 ♘h2 ♘g8 14 f4

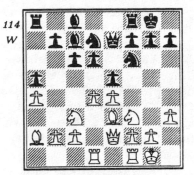

f6 15 ♕g4 ed 16 ♗xd4 ♘c5 17 f5 ♘xb3 18 ♕xg6+± worked out very well for White in the game Alekhine - Marco. Stockholm 1912; Black's play was pathetic) 9 ... ♘h7 10 ♗e3 ♗f6 11 ♖fd1 ♕e7 12 ♕c4 ♖e8 13 a5 ♘hf8 14 d5 c5 15 ♘b5 ♘b8 *(115)*

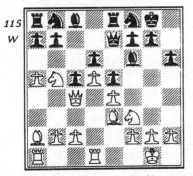

16 ♗xc5! dc 17 d6 ♕d7 18 ♘c7 b5 19 ♕d5 1-0 Bogoljubov - Seleniev, Triberg 1916.

9 h3

I have my doubts about the efficacy of **9 a5!?** i.e: 9 ... ♖b8 (with the intention of continuing 10 ... b5 11 ab ab and 12 ... b5 again) 10 ♗e3 ♘g4! (and why not?) 11

♗d2 ♘gf6 12 h3 b5 13 ab ab and if 14 d5? b5 15 ♗b3 b4 16 ♘a4 cd∓ or 15 dc? bc 16 cd ♗xd7∓; but not the immediate 10 ... b5? as 11 ab ab 12 d5 b5 13 ♖a7 ♗b7 14 dc bc 15 ♘d5! ♘xd5 16 ed± - analysis by Pickett, the bishop on e3 makes all the difference.

If **9 ♗a2** (better than 9 ♗b3 which encourages: 9 ... a6!? 10 h3 ed!? 11 ♘xd4 ♖e8 - gaining an important tempo - 12 ♗f4 ♗f8 13 f3 ♘c5 14 ♗a2 ♘e6 15 ♗xe6 ♗xe6 16 ♕d2 ♖ad8 17 ♖fe1 ♗c8 18 ♖ad1 ♘d7! 19 ♘f5 ♘e5 20 ♘d4 f6 21 ♔h1 ♕f7 with a fine position for Black, Teichmann - Nimzowitsch, Carlsbad 1911) then 9 ... b6 10 ♗e3 ♘g4 11 ♗d2 ♘gf6 12 h3 a6 is possible, or 10 ... a6, but not 10 ... ♗b7?! as it is no longer possible to defend f5: 11 ♘h4! ed (11 ... g6? 12 de de 13 ♗h6 ♖fe8 14 ♗xf7+ ♔xf7 15 ♕c4+±) 12 ♗xd4 c5 13 ♗e3 ♘xe4 14 ♘f5 ♗f6? (14 ... ♘df6 15 ♘b5 ♕d7 16 ♘xe7+ ♕xe7 17 f3 a6 was less clear) 15 ♘d5 ♗xd5 16 ♗xd5± Zaitsev - Durao, Sochi 1977.

9 ... b6
This is the best, intending ... a6, and a later ... b5, when Black will have something worthwhile on the queenside. 9 ... ed?! seems out of place here: 10 ♘xd4 ♖e8 11 ♗f4 ♘e5 12 ♗b3 ♘fd7 13 ♖ad1 ♗f8 14 ♗c1!? ♘c5 15 ♗a2 d5? 16 f4 ♘ed7 17 e5 ♘b6 18 a5 ♘bd7 19 ♕h5 with a strong attack, Grefe - Najdorf, Lone Pine 1976.

10 ♖d1
10 ♗e3 is also met by 10 ... a6, and not 10 ... ♗b7 11 de de 12 ♘h4 ♗c5 13 ♖ad1 ♖ad8 14 ♗g5 h6 15 ♖xd7! ♘xd7 16 ♕h5, Zhidkov - Kogan, USSR 1969.

10 ... a6!
Setting up the desired queenside pawn structure. It is still a mistake to play 10 ... ♗b7 as 11 de de 12 ♘h4 ♖fe8 13 ♘f5 ♗f8 14 ♕f3 is most unpleasant, Klompus - Schermann, Corr 1961/63; although 11 ... ♘xe5 is better, ±.

Black should have fair chances after 10 ... a6: 11 de?! de 12 ♘h4 ♘c5 13 ♕f3 ♗e6 14 ♗xe6 ♘xe6 15 ♘f5 ♖fd8= (Pickett); or 11 ♗g5 ♗b7 12 ♘h4 g6= (Cafferty); or finally 11 ♗e3 ♗b7 12 de de 13 ♘h4 ♘c5 14 ♕f3 b5∓.

B
7 ♖e1
Arguably the best of the seventh move alternatives. While bolsters e4 and will react according to the deployment of Black's forces. Whilst 7 ♖e1 is not as vigorous as 7 ♕e2.

neither does it suffer the disadvantages of 7 ♕e2; and it restricts Black's activity to a minimum.

7 ... c6

8 a4

White must restrain Black's queenside expansion. Of course, 8 ♗b3 is met, not by 8 ... ed? 9 ♕xd4 ♘c5 10 h3 ♘e6 11 ♕e3 ♘c7±, Blake - Wahltuch, Liverpool 1923, but by 8 ... b5 and if 9 d5?! b4 10 dc bc 11 cd ♗b7∓.

8 ... b6!

It is probably best to dispense with ... ♕c7 and get on with the queenside play; there is no pressing need to remove the queen from the d-file. Formerly, Black has played more routinely:

a) **8 ... ♕c7** 9 h3 (9 ♗g5 ed? 10 ♘xd4 ♘e5 11 ♗f1 ♖e8 12 h3 ♘fd7 13 ♗e3 ♗f8 14 ♕d2 ♘c5 15 ♖ad1 g6? 16 ♘db5!, with the idea of 16 ... cb 17 ♘d5 ♕d8 18 ♗g5 and 19 ♘f6++-, Ernevoldsen - Nilssen, Danish Ch 1955; or 9 ♗d2!? ♘b6 10 ♗a2 ♗g4 11 a5 ♘bd7 12 d5 cd 13 ♗xd5±, Hort - Ree, Wijk aan Zee 1979; finally, 9 a5!? ♖b8!? 10 d5 b5 11 ab ♘xb6 12 ♗b3 cd∞, or 12 ♗a6? ♗xa6 13 ♖xa6 ♕b7∓; and 9 b3 b6 10 ♗b2 a6=) 9 ... b6 (9 ... h6 did well in the game Darcyl - Bernat: 10 ♗e3 ♖e8 11 ♕d2

♗f8 12 ♖ad1 a6 13 b4? b5 14 ab cb 15 ♗d3 ♗b7 16 d5 ♖ac8 17 ♘b1 ♘xd5! 18 ed e4∓ but White's play was a big help) 10 ♗g5 a6 11 d5, but instead of 11 ... ♗b7 12 dc ♗xc6 13 ♕e2 ♗b7 14 ♖ad1 ♖fc8 15 b3 g6 16 ♗xf6 ♘xf6, Piket - Ree, Dutch Ch 1990, 17 ♘h2-g4±; 11 ... c5 was possible, with a Benoni-type formation.

b) **8 ... a5** 9 h3 ♕e8!? (playing Pickett's plan here seems quite solid; 9 ... ed?! 10 ♘xd4 ♘c5 11 ♗f4 ♖e8 12 ♕f3 ♗f8 13 ♖ad1 ♘cd7 14 ♗b3 g6 15 g4 ♕e7 16 ♘xc6! bc 17 ♗xd6 was better for White in Tukmakov - Planinc, Amsterdam 1974) 10 ♗a2 ♘d8 11 ♗e3 ♕e7 12 ♕d2 ♘c7 12 ♖ad1 ♘b6±, A Sokolov - Loheac, Dubai Olympiad 1986.

9 h3

If White is seeking the advantage he must play 9 d5! and now: 9 ... ♗b7 (9 ...c5!? is untried but seems to me like Black's best, e.g. 10 a5 a6! 11 ab ♘xb6 with the intention of continuing ... ♘e8 - c7 - b5 and then playing for ... f5∞, but possibly ∓!) 10 dc ♗xc6 11 ♗g5 a6 (in this Sicilian-type position, White will want to take on f6 anyway to try and gain control of the d5 square, therefore it is a waste of time to play 11 ...

h6?! 12 ♗xf6 ♘xf6 13 ♕d3 g6 14 ♘d2 ♔g7 15 ♗d5 ♘xd5 16 ♘xd5± Kindermann – Plachetka, Trnava 1987) 12 ♗xf6 ♘xf6 13 ♘d5! ♘xd5 14 ♗xd5 ♖c8 15 c3 ♕c7 16 ♗xc6 ♕xc6 17 ♕d3 (White would like to transport his knight to d5, but not only is this time-consuming, it is not so easy to win when it does get there. I once lost a position like this, with the knight on d5, to Grandmaster Murray Chandler. There is more than a grain of truth in Tartakower's saying that 'the worst bishop is better than the best knight') 17 ... ♕c4 18 ♖ed1 ♕xd3 19 ♖xd3 f5 (counterplay) 20 ♘d2 g6 21 ♖e1 ♖c6 22 g3 ♔f7 23 f4!? ef 24 gf ♗f6 25 ♖h3 ♔g8 26 ef gf 27 ♔f2 b5!= 28 ab ab 29 ♘f3 ♖c4 30 ♖d1 ♖xf4 31 ♖xd6 b4 32 cb ♖xb4 33 ♖d2 ♖xb2 *(116)*

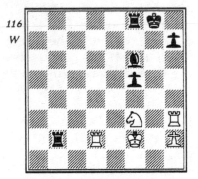

(suddenly the bishop makes its presence felt!) 34 ♖xb2 ♗xb2 when Black was a

pawn to the good, although the reduced material meant that a draw was almost inevitable, Jansa - Mokry, Trnava 1987.

9   ...   a6
10   ♗g5

10 d5 has less force here as Black can simply reply ... c5 (White no longer has the follow-up a5) with a Czech-Benoni type position, where White's possibilities are restricted. Normally, Black would prepare the move ... f5 by way of ... ♘e8, ... g6, ... ♘g7, ... ♔h8, ... ♘f6-g8 etc, remembering to exchange dark-squared bishops, if he should get the chance, by way of ... ♗g5.

In the game Schmidt - Andanov, Warsaw 1987, White decided to re-position his bishop: **10 ♗f1 ♗b7 11 g3 ♖e8 12 ♗g2 ♕b8 13 ♗e3∞**, but simply 11 ... b5 was fine. In my game against the Bulgarian GM Krum Georgiev, Torcy 1991, some interesting tactics occurred after **10 ♗e3 ♗b7 11 ♗b3 b5 12 ♘d2 ed!? 13 ♗xd4 c5 14 ♗xf6 ♗xf6 15 ♗d5 ♗xc3 16 ♗xb7 ♗xb2 17 ♖a2 ♖b8 18 ♗xa6 ba 19 ♖xa4=** and at this point he offered a draw. As he was already an hour behind on the clock (a common occurrence in my games with

the Philidor) I declined, although it was a draw some
25 moves later, anyway!

10	...	♗b7
11	♗b3	b5
12	ab	ab
13	♖xa8	♗xa8
14	♕e2	♕c7
15	♗h4	h6 *(117)*

117
W

The opening has been a
success for Black, and the
position is level. Now
comes a period of man-
oeuvring where both sides
try to improve the pros-
pects of their respective
pieces. Black decides to
play ... ♖e8, ... g6 and ...
♗g7, but first he has to
stop White replying ♘g5,
so he plays ... h6. It is interesting to note that he
chooses to play this at a
moment when White is un-
able to play ♘h4-f5.

16	♘d1	♖e8
17	c3	♗f8
18	♗c2	♗b7
19	de	de
20	♘e3	g6
21	♖d1	♗g7

22 ♘g4?!

A harmless enough
looking move, but the
slight weakness that White
has created on his kingside
is exploited by Black in an
interesting fashion.

22	...	♘xg4
23	hg	♗c8
24	♘d2	g5!
25	♗g3	♘f6
26	f3	h5
27	♕e3	

This is better than 27 gh?
♘xh5 28 ♗f2 ♘f4 29 ♕e3
g4∓ or 28 ♗h2 ♘f4 29 ♗xf4
gf∓.

27	...	hg
28	♕xg5	♘h7
29	♕e3	♖e6
30	fg?	

It would have been bett-
er to play 30 f4 ef 31 ♗xf4
♗e5 32 g3, although White
is still worse. It is noticeable that as soon as White
has made a slip, the black
pieces swarm out. The attack proceeds very smoothly
from here on in.

30	...	♗h6
31	♕e2	♖g6
32	♘f3	♗xg4
33	♕d3	♗xf3!
34	♕xf3	♘f6
35	♗b3	♘g4
36	♖d3	♗f4!
37	♗xf4	ef
38	♕d1 *(118)*	

38 ... f3 looks like a killer
here: 39 ♖xf3? ♕h2+ 40 ♔f1
♕h1+ 41 ♔e2 ♕xg2+ or 39

118
B

♕xf3 ♕h2+ 40 ♔f1 ♖f6 or 39 ♗xf7+ ♕xf7 40 ♖d8+ ♔h7 41 ♖d7 f2+ 42 ♔f1 ♘e3+ but, in this last line, 40 ♖xf3 permits White a little more resistance. The line chosen by Black is clear enough: 38 ... ♕b6+ 39 ♖d4 c5 40 ♖d8+ ♔g7 41 ♗xf7!? c4+ 42 ♕d4+ ♕xd4+ 43 cd ♔xf7 44 ♖b8 ♖a6 (Black is still attacking, mate in one is the threat!) 45 ♔f1 ♖a2 46 ♖xb5 c3 47 bc ♘e3+ 48 ♔g1 ♖xg2+ 49 ♔h1 f3 50 ♖b1 ♘g4 0-1, Antunes - Cifuentes, Dubai Olympiad 1986, ... ♘f2 mate is rather decisive.

A near perfect example of Black's best strategy against 7 ♖e1 - calm strategical play, but ready to punish White should he overpress. Capturing on d4 never seems to equalize for Black in this line.

C

7   a4 (without ♖e1)
A flexible continuation - as White will play this

anyway, why not immediately?

7   ...   c6
8   a5

This is an idea that we have seen before - White attempts to cramp Black on the queenside. 8 ♕e2?! ed! transposes to A21 and 8 ♖e1 to B; 8 ♗a2 is a useful move, but it leads to positions of a type that we have previously examined e.g: 8 ... ♕c7 (*8 ... ed?!* is still of doubtful value: *9 ♘xd4 ♘c5 10 ♖e1 a5 11 h3 ♖e8 12 ♕f3 ♗f8?! 13 ♗g5 ♘e6 14 ♘xe6! ♗xe6 15 e5 ♗xa2.* 15 ... de 16 ♖ed1 ♕e7 17 ♘e4±. *16 ef ♗e6 17 fg! ♗e7 18 ♗xe7 ♕xe7 19 ♘e4 f5 20 ♘g3 ♕xg7 21 ♕f4!*, Ciocaltea - Mohring, Halle 1974, with a miserable position for Black. It is possible to play as in B, however, with *8 ... b6!* followed by ... a6, ... ♗b7, ... b5. Two examples: *9 ♕e2 ♗b7?!* 9 ... a6! first is best, it is important to continue controlling f5, as we shall see. *10 ♖d1 ♕c7 11 ♘h4.* Better than 11 de de 12 ♘h4 ♘c5 13 ♘f5 ♗c8 - sic - 14 ♕f3 ♗xf5 15 ♕xf5 ♖ad8= Cifuentes - Adams, Buenos Aires 1991. *11 ... ed? 12 ♖xd4 ♖fe8 13 ♗f4 ♗f8 14 ♖ad1 ♘e5±* Fedorowicz - Cifuentes, Buenos Aires 1991. Interestingly, the actual move order of the Adams game was 8 ...

Ħe8 9 ♘g5 Ħf8 10 ♘f3 Ħe8 11 ♘g5 Ħf8 12 ♘f3 and only then 12 ... b6, disdaining the draw! Black should be careful to defend his queen's rook before playing ... b5 as White can play ♗xf7+ in some variations, winning the rook) 9 h3 (9 Ħe1 is, again, similar to variation B, one example: 9 ... b6 10 ♗e3 a6 11 ♘h4 ed 12 ♕xd4 ♘c5 13 b4 ♘g4?! – 13 ... ♘e6 14 ♕d1 g6∞ was preferable – 14 ♘f5 ♗f6 15 e5± Vogt – Hesse, East Germany 1986. Rather than allowing White to play 10 ♗e3 without h3, as here, I think that Black should play ... ♘g4, for instance: 10 ... ♘g4!? 11 ♗d2 ♘gf6!? – or 11 ... a6 12 h3 ♘gf6 – as the bishop is not well placed on d2 and will probably have to move again soon) 9 ... b6 10 Ħe1 a6 11 ♘h4 Ħe8 12 ♘f5 ♗f8 13 ♗e3 ♗b7 14 de de 15 ♕f3 b5±, Parma – Barendregt, Amsterdam 1965, but 11 ... g6 was not beyond the bounds of possibility.

8 ... h6?!

Actually this is not a very good move. I have chosen this game, however, to demonstrate how resilient Hanham's variation is in the hands of a strong player. After all, everyone plays the occasional bad move, but this need not be

the end of the story!

Some alternatives: 8 ... ♕c7 9 ♗a2 (9 Ħe1 h6 10 h3 Ħe8 11 ♗e3 ♘f8 12 d5?! – Karpov was very young when he played this, I'm sure that nowadays he would pefer something like 12 ♗a2, maintaining the tension – 12 ... cd 13 ♗xd5 ♘xd5 14 ♘xd5 ♕d8 15 c4±, Karpov – Noakh, USSR 1966. 9 ... Ħb8 was a better solution for Black, 10 h3 b5 11 ab ab=) 9 ... ed (not a bad idea as White's a4 – a5 doesn't contribute to his development, but 9 ... Ħb8 and ... b5 was again equal) 10 ♘xd4 Ħe8 11 ♘f5 (11 Ħe1 ♗f8 12 h3 ♘c5 13 ♕f3?! d5!) 11 ... ♗f8 12 ♘g3 ♘c5 13 Ħe1 ♗e6= Ostojic – Ree, Budapest 1977.

If 8 ... Ħb8 9 ♕e2 then 9 ... ♕c7! 10 h3 b5 11 ab ab 12 d5? b5 13 dc bc 14 cd ♗xd7∓ is better than the immediate 9 ... b5?! as 10 ab ab 11 d5 b5 12 dc bc 13 cd ♗xd7 14 ♕xc4 wins a pawn.

9	♗a2	Ħe8
10	de	de
11	♕e2	♗f8
12	Ħd1	♕c7
13	♘h4	♘c5

White certainly seems to have a good deal of pressure on the kingside, but against Black's defensive skill it just evaporates.

14	♘f5	♔h7

15	♕f3	♘g8
16	b4	♘e6
17	♖b1?	

Stein considers 17 b5 with the idea of a5-a6, trying to gain control of d5, to be better, but 17 ... g6 18 ♘e3 ♗b4 is more than adequate.

17	...	g6
18	♘e3	♗g7
19	♘c4	♘d4
20	♕d3	♖d8
21	♕f1	♗e6 *(119)*

The white pieces have been driven back, the black knight has taken up the powerful post on d4, Black is better. And White was one of the strongest attacking players of all time!

22 ♘e3 ½-½

Stein - Petrosian, Moscow 1971. Presumably Black had decided to make a draw that day.

D

Other White 7th moves

None of these moves are in any way critical tests of Black's set up; but whilst they are not exactly disastrous for White, they do imply a faulty appreciation of the position that very often results in White committing further inaccuracies that really are fatal.

a) 7 ♗e3 c6 8 ♗b3?! (8 a4 is, of course, the right move, when 8 ... ♘g4 9 ♗d2 ♘b6 10 ♗b3 ed 11 ♘xd4 ♗f6 12 ♘f5 ♗xf5 13 ef ♘e5 is a possibility) 8 ... b5 (the natural response, but 8 ... ♘g4 9 ♗d2 ed 10 ♘xd4 ♘c5 is also good) 9 ♘d2 (9 d5?! is best answered by 9 ... b4! 10 dc bc 11 cd ♗b7∓; although 9 ... c5 10 ♘xb5 ♘xe4 11 ♘d2 a6 12 ♘a3 ♘xd2 13 ♕xd2 f5 is also interesting, Romanovsky - Ilyin-Zhenevsky, Leningrad 1921) 9 ... a6 10 ♘e2 ♗b7 11 c3 c5!? 12 d5 c4∓, Gutgilf - Romanovsky, Moscow 1923 (13 ♗c2 ♘g4 is rather awkward).

b) 7 de?! de. As Black can only take on d4 and concede the centre if there is a tactical justification, likewise White can only capture on e5 if it is part of a well-conceived tactical operation. The resultant central configuration slightly favours Black, if anyone, as he has pawn control of d5, whilst White cannot say the same about d4. Obviously, there is no good reason to take on e5 at this juncture; Black gains use of b4 and c5, while White gains nothing: 8 ♗g5 c6 9 a4 ♕c7 10 ♕e2 (or 10 ♘h4 ♘c5 11 ♘f5 ♗xf5 12 ef ♖ad8 13 ♕e2 ♘d5 Valli - Laplaza, 1970) 10 ... ♘c5 11 ♘e1? ♘e6 12 ♗e3 ♘d4!∓ Evenson - Alekhine, Kiev 1916.

c) **7 h3** c6 8 a4 (8 a3?! b5 9 ♗a2 ♗b7 10 de?! de 11 ♕e2 a5 12 ♖d1 ♕c7 13 ♗g5 ♘c5 14 ♗xf6?! ♗xf6∓ Rosetto - Guimard, Argentina 1969; 8 de?! de 9 ♕e2?! b5 10 ♗d3 ♕c7∓ Bonch-Osmalovsky - Chistiakov, Moscow 1950) 8 ... b6! (8 ... ♘xe4? worked very well in Perez - Ortega, Cuba 1963: 9 ♘xe4 d5 10 ♗d3? de 11 ♗xe4 f5 12 ♗d3 e4 13 ♗c4+ ♔h8 14 ♘e5 ♘xe5 15 de ♕e8 16 ♗f4 g5 17 ♗d2 f4 with a dangerous attack. Simply 10 ♘xe5 is better for White, though: 10 ... ♘xe5 11 de dc 12 ♘d6 ♗xd6 13 ed, or 11 ... de 12 ♗f4 ♗f5 13 ♕e2, and not 10 ... dc? 11 ♘xc4 winning a pawn) 9 ♗e3 a6 10 d5?! (we have seen this advance before. As I mentioned then, it is better for Black to play ... c5 with a Czech-Benoni formation, than ... ♗b7. Here is an example of what might happen) 10 ... c5! 11 g4?! (as the centre is closed, White decides to

advance on the kingside. Whether he intended to attack here, or merely wanted to make it difficult for Black to play ... f5, I don't know. In fact g4 is a common idea in the main Czech-Benoni; but here Black is able to exploit the weakening of the dark-squares with a series of accurate moves. The French grand-master Renet played more sensibly against me at Franconville 1991: 11 ♘d2 ♘e8 12 ♗e2, intending ♘c4 with unclear play, although Black later won this important last round game) 11 ... h5! 12 ♘d2 hg 13 hg ♘h7 14 ♔g2 ♗g5 (exchanging the defender of the f4 square) 15 ♕e2 ♗xe3 16 ♕xe3 ♖e8 17 ♖h1 ♘df8 18 f3 ♘g6∓ *(120)*

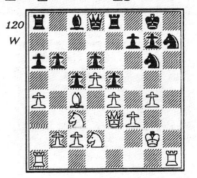

120
W

Hon - Cifuentes, Dubai Olympiad 1986. Not only has Black the advantage on the kingside (knights coming to f4 and g5), but also on the queenside where he can prepare the ... b5 break.

d) 7 ♗g5?! (the bishop is misplaced here, but it is the sort of 'active' move that weaker players are very fond of) 7 ... c6 8 ♕e2?! (8 a4 is better; 8 ♗b3 b5 9 a3 ♗b7 10 ♖e1 a6= Rahman – Bell, Southampton 1986. The text transposes into one of the classic Hanham games, played by, arguably, its greatest connoisseur, Aron Nimzowitsch) 8 ... h6 9 ♗h4?! ♘h5 (forcing the exchange of a piece; as a general rule exchanges favour the side with least space – in this case Black – and therefore it would have been better for White to retreat his bishop to e3, say, instead) 10 ♗g3 ♘xg3 11 hg b5 12 ♗d3 a6 13 a4 ♗b7 (121) (Black has achieved his ideal queenside set-up, and has the bishop pair)

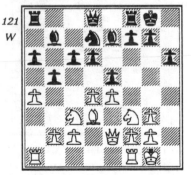

14 ♖ad1 ♕c7 15 ab ab 16 g4 ♖fe8 17 d5 b4 18 dc ♗xc6 19 ♘b1 ♘c5 20 ♘bd2 ♕c8 21 ♗c4 g6 22 g3 ♔g7 23 ♘h2 ♗g5 (the threat to the e-

pawn forces a fresh king-side weakness. The importance of this will become clear very soon) 24 f3 ♕c7 25 ♖fe1 (122)

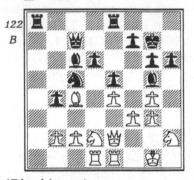

(Black's pieces seem to have found their optimum positions, the question is: How best to proceed?) 25 ... ♖h8! (the white kingside pawns are very static, and he can do nothing about Black levering open the h-file) 26 ♘df1 h5 27 gh ♖xh5 28 ♗d5 ♖ah8 29 ♗xc6 ♕xc6 30 ♕c4 ♕b6 31 ♔g2 ♘e6 32 ♖e2 ♘d4 33 ♖ee1 ♕b7 (the game is all but over; Black menaces ... ♕d7-h3+ and ... ♖c8. White decides to give up the exchange, but he can't convert a bad position into a good one) 34 ♖xd4 cd 35 ♘g4 ♕b6 36 f4 ♗e7 37 ♖d1 f5 38 ♘f2 fe 39 ♕xd4+ ♕xd4 40 ♖xd4 d5 41 g4 ♗c5 42 ♖d1 ♖h4 winning easily, Teichmann – Nimzowitsch, San Sebastian 1911. Superb!

In conclusion, in these variations, Black should

attempt to expand on the queen's wing, but should be prepared to capture in the centre and initiate tactical play at an opportune moment. The theory of restraint is as valid today as it was when first proposed by Nimzowitsch, but, be careful, it is not a panacea!

10) Exchange Variation

1	e4	e5
2	♘f3	d6
3	d4	♘f6
4	de *(123)*	

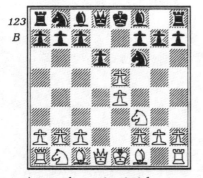

A rather insipid move. Instead of keeping the tension with ♘c3, White captures on e5. After the further, inevitable, exchange of the white pawn on e5 for the black pawn on d6 a position is reached where both central files are open.

Despite the drawish nature of the resultant positions, White possesses a small lead in development and therefore Black must take a certain amount of care.

4	...	♘xe4

There are now two main possibilities.

A 5 ♕d5!
B 5 ♘bd2

Alternatively, **5 ♗d3?!** ♘c5 6 0-0 ♗e7 7 ♗e3 ♘xd3 8 ♕xd3 de 9 ♘xe5 ♕xd3 10 ♘xd3 0-0 11 ♗c5 (in order to relieve Black of the bishop pair; 11 ♘c3 ♘a6! 12 ♘d5 ♗d8 13 ♘c5 b6 14 ♘xa6 ♗xa6 is no better, since whereas White's initiative is of a temporary nature. Once Black deals with the immediate threats the white pieces will be driven back and Black's two bishops promise him a permanent initiative) 11 ... ♗xc5 12 ♘xc5 b6∓, as the black bishop will be the dominant minor piece.

5 ♗c4! c6! (the threat is ... d5, winning a tempo at the expense of the bishop on c4, e.g. 6 0-0 d5 7 ♗d3 ♘c5 8 ♗g5 ♗e7 9 ♗xe7 ♕xe7 10 c4 dc 11 ♗xc4 0-0= as in Sozin - Romanovsky, Novgorod 1923, but the ambitious player of the black pieces might prefer the more combative 8 ... ♕b6!? planning ... ♗g4, ... ♘e6, ... ♗c5, ... 0-0, ... ♘d7 etc) 6 ed ♘xd6 (this is better than 6 ... ♗xd6 7 0-0 0-0 8 ♕d4 as the black knight on e4 serves only as a target for White) 7 ♗b3 ♗e7 8 0-0 0-0 9 ♘c3 ♘a6! is very pleasant for Black, who threatens ... ♘c5 (xb3) and can answer 10 ♗e3 with ... ♘f5.

A

     5   ♕d5!

This is the only move that offers White any hope of keeping a real advantage.

     5   ...   ♘c5

It would not be a good idea to try to maintain the knight on e4 by 5 ... f5 as, although ... c6 and ... d5 is a threat, the obvious and rather brutal 6 ♗c4 forces 6 .. ♕e7 (6 ... ♕d7? 7 e6, when 7 ... ♕e7 8 ♕xf5 and 7 ... ♕c6?? 8 ♗b5) tangling up the black pieces.

     6   ♗g5

The only relevant move. 6 ♘g5 ♘e6!? (Steiner – Alekhine, Podebrady 1936 featured the more forcing 6 ... ♗e6! 7 ♘xe6 fe 8 ♕f3 ♘bd7 9 ed ♗xd6 10 ♘c3 ♕h4, when White has a strategic advantage, but is somewhat behind in development: 11 g3? ♘e5 12 ♕e2

♕f6 13 f4 ♘c6 14 ♗e3 0-0-0 15 0-0-0 e5! 16 fe ♗xe5! *(124)*

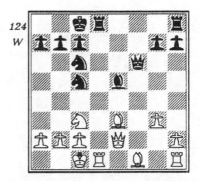

17 ♘d5 – 17 ♗xc5 ♗xc3 18 bc ♕xc3-+ – 17 ... ♗xb2+ 18 ♔b1 ♕e5 19 ♕g4+ ♘d7 20 ♗f4 ♕e4 21 ♗b5 ♘d4 when Black was better) 7 ♘e4 (7 ♗c4? c6, but 7 ♘xe6 is more of a problem: 7 ... ♗xe6!? 8 ♕xb7 ♘d7 9 ed ♗xd6 10 ♗e2 0-0 may not offer Black enough compensation for the pawn, so 7 ... fe may be superior: 8 ♕f3 d5 is unclear; Black hopes to play it like a French Defence with ... c5, ... ♘c6 etc, but 9 ♗d3 is a problem) 7 ... de 8 ♕xe5 ♗e7 9 ♘c3 ♘c6=.

Alternatively **6 ed** ♕xd6?! 7 ♘c3 ♗e7 8 ♕xd6 ♗xd6 9 ♘b5 ♘c6 10 ♘xd6+, Karklins – Deverett, Chicago 1989, is a good example of how not to play the black side of this position; simply 6 ... ♗xd6 7 ♗g5 f6 8 ♗e3 ♗e6 is fine.

After **6 ♗g5** there is a choice between

A1 6 ... ♕d7!? and
A2 6 ... ♗e7

A1

6 ... ♕d7!? *(125)*

The queen move looks ugly but is probably best here.

7 ed

Further releasing the tension, but 7 ♘c3 c6 8 ♕d2 de 9 ♘xe5 ♕xd2+ 10 ♗xd2 ♗e6 11 0-0-0 ♘bd7 12 ♘f3, Velimirovic - V Nikolic, Bela Crkva 1984, is best countered by 12 ... ♗g4 13 ♖e1+ ♘e6 14 ♘d4 ♗c5! which should peter out to equality. A more ambitious player might prefer 8 ... d5!?, intending to continue with ... ♘e6 and, possibly, ... ♗b4.

7 ... ♗xd6
8 ♘c3 0-0
9 0-0-0 ♘c6

Petrosian's move. Black should, of course, be endeavouring to make good his arrears in development as quickly as possible. For this reason, moves such as 9 ... a6? 10 ♗e3 ♘e6 11 ♘e5 and 9 ... ♕g4? 10 h3 ♕h5 11 ♗e2, with advantage to White in both cases, are insufficient. However, 9 ... h6 10 ♗e3 ♕e7 may be playable, when ... ♗e6 is a threat, hitting White's exposed queen.

10 ♗e3

Chandler's suggestion of 10 ♘b5 seems more critical.

10 ... ♘e7
11 ♕c4

11 ♕d2 is also a possibility.

11 ... b6!
12 ♗xc5

This is quoted as an improvement over the 12 ♘e4 of Byrne - Petrosian, Manila 1976, which continued: 12 ... ♘xe4 13 ♕xe4 ♕c6 14 ♗d3 ♕xe4 15 ♗xe4 ♖b8 16 ♘d4 ♗d7 17 ♗he1 ½-½. The position is level, but there is no reason why either player shouldn't consider playing on here - there are lots of pieces left on the board. Black can place his rooks on the central files and proceed from there, ... f7-f4 at the right time will push the adversary back.

12 ... bc

Despite having his queenside pawn structure compromised in this way, Black does have the bishop pair and use of the b-file in compensation.

13 ♗d3 ♖b8!

The queen's rook obviously belongs on this file, in the meantime there is a threat of ... ♖b4 winning on the spot.

14 ♘e4

14 ♗xh7+? ♔xh7 15 ♕h4+ ♔g8 16 ♘g5 ♕f5 defends h7 and refutes the attack; 14 ♕h4 ♘g6 (or 14 ... ♘f5) 15 ♗xg6 fg! should be to Black's advantage.

14 ... ♕c6

15 ♘xd6 cd

White manages to exchange Black's bishop like this, but he strengthens his pawn structure at the same time. Bearing in mind that Black is now menacing ... d5 and ... ♗e6, not to mention ... ♕b6, White's next may be obligatory.

16 ♕e4 ♕xe4

17 ♗xe4 ♖d8

18 ♖he1 h6 (*126*)

The extra black centre pawn gives him very slightly the better chances.

A2

6 ... ♗e7

With best play for both sides, this appears to lead to a tiny endgame advantage for White. From Black's viewpoint, he may have quite a long struggle ahead of him before he gets a draw, and his winning chances seem limited.

Incidentally, 6 ... f6 is also legal, but is certainly not to be recommended, 7 ef gf 8 ♗e3±.

7 ed ♕xd6

8 ♘c3 h6 (*127*)

In my opinion, the best chance. If the bishop moves to e3 the e-file will be blocked, if only temporarily. There are many other possibilities, mostly indifferent:

a) **8 ... c6** 9 ♕xd6 ♗xd6 10 0-0-0 ♗e7 11 ♗c4! ♗e6 12 ♖he1 ♘ba6 13 ♗xe7 ♔xe7 14 ♘d4 Adler - Chistyakov, Leningrad 1963, leaves Black a grim defensive task ahead of him.

b) **8 ... ♗e6** 9 ♕xd6 ♗xd6 10 ♘b5! ♘c6 11 ♘xd6+ cd 12 0-0-0 0-0 13 ♗e3 (not 13 ♖xd6? ♘e4 and ... ♘xf2) 13 ... ♖ac8 14 a3 ♘e4 15 ♘d4 Lublinsky - Schonmann, USSR - Germany Corr 1960 and although Black won this game, his position is markedly inferior at this juncture.

c) **8 ... ♕xd5** is the second best move: 9 ♘xd5 ♗d6 10 0-0-0 ♘c6 (10 ... 0-0? 11 ♗e7! ♗xe7 12 ♘xe7+ ♚h8 13 ♘xc8 ♖xc8 14 ♗c4 f6 15 ♖he1±) 11 ♗b5 ♗d7 12 ♖he1+ ♘e6 13 c4±, Sadomsky - Abroshin, Corr 1954, though White must achieve something concrete soon as Black will quickly castle and catch up on his development, when the position should be equal.

9 ♗e3 c6

Now is not the time to play 9 ... ♕xd5? 10 ♘xd5 (as 10 ... ♗d6?? 11 ♗xc5 ♗xc5 12 ♘xc7+ would be a catastrophe) Morgado - Palmo, Axelson Memorial Corr 1989, continued: 10 ... ♘e6 11 ♘xe7 ♚xe7 12 ♘d4 ♖e8 13 0-0-0 ♘xd4 14 ♗xd4 ♚f8 15 ♗b5 ♘c6 16 ♗c5+ ♚g8 17 ♗xc6?!. I can't agree with this. Of course, Black now has chronically weak queenside pawns but the opposite-coloured bishops will make it very difficult

for White to win. I believe that White should keep both bishops and gradually increase the pressure; as it is White never did win any of the queenside pawns and the game was later drawn.

10 ♕xd6 ♗xd6
11 0-0-0 ♘e7
12 ♗c4 ♘ba6
13 ♖he1 ♗e6
14 ♘e5?

Gipslis indicates that 14 ♗xe6 ♘xe6 15 ♘e4 ♘b4 16 ♘c5 is clearly better for White, but 16 ... ♘xa2+ 17 ♚b1 ♘b4 18 ♘xb7 ♘d5 might not be so awful e.g: 19 ♗c5? ♖b8∓ or 19 ♘a5 ♘xe3, which is only a slight edge to White.

14 ... 0-0
15 ♗xe6 ♘xe6
16 f4 ♖fd8
17 ♖xd8+ ♗xd8
18 f5 ♘f8

And in the game Smit - Peterson, USSR 1972, Black soon managed to achieve a draw.

Personally speaking, I would not fancy playing any of the endgames after 6 ... ♗e7; chess should be more fun!

B

5 ♘bd2

This should give Black fewer problems than the previous line; he has the choice between playing the simple, and good, 5 ... ♘xd2 or the more complicated 5 ... ♘c5.

B1 5 ... ♘xd2
B2 5 ... ♘c5

Both **5 ... f5?** 6 ♘xe4 fe 7 ♘g5 d5 8 e6, which transposes into an inferior variation of Mestel's line, and **5 ... ♗f5** 6 ♕e2 d5 7 ♘d4 ♗g6 8 ♕b5+ are terrible for Black, so it is evident that he will not be able to maintain his knight on e4, which brings us to:

B1

| 5 | ... | ♘xd2 |
| 6 | ♗xd2 | ♗e7 |

This is the most common reply, 6... de 7 ♗c4 ♗e7 8 ♘xe5 0-0 9 ♕h5± is clearly bad, but what is wrong with 6 ... ♘c6, putting pressure on e5? There is very little practical experience with this move as yet, but here are several possibilities:

a) **7 ed?!** ♗xd6 8 ♗d3 0-0 9 0-0 (9 ♗xh7+? ♔xh7 10 ♘g5+ ♔g8 11 ♕h5 ♗f5-+) 9 ... ♗g4 and Black is at least equal e.g: 10 h3 ♗h5 11 ♗c3 (note that, whilst the black queen is on d8, 11 ♗xh7+? ♔xh7 12 ♘g5+ is answered by 12 ... ♕xg5-+) 11 ... ♖e8 12 ♗e2 ♖e4!? and ... ♕e7

b) **7 ♗b5** ♗d7 (7 ... a6 8 ♗xc6+ bc is also playable) 8 ♕e2 (8 ed ♗xd6 is easy for Black, and 8 ♗f4 is met by 8 ... ♘xe5) 8 ... ♘xe5 9 ♘xe5 de 10 0-0-0 (10 ♕xe5+ ♕e7=) 10 ... ♗d6 should be OK.

c) **7 ♗c3** d5 8 ♕d2 ♗e6 looks fairly equal, but Schonmann managed to win this position as Black a couple of times in the Europa cup Corr 1959/60.

d) **7 ♗f4** d5 8 ♗d3 ♗e7±/= might be White's best.

7 ♗d3

7 ed ♕xd6 8 ♗c3 0-0 9 ♕xd6 ♗xd6 10 0-0-0 ♗g4 doesn't inconvenience Black in the slightest, Boleslavsky – Keres, Moscow 1962. and 7 ♗f4 d5 8 ♗d3 c5 9 c3 ♘c6 10 h3 (10 ♕e2 ♗e6 11 0-0 occurred in Levin – Chernin, USSR 1969, where Black continued 11 ... g5!? 12 ♗d2 g4 13 ♘e1 ♕b6 14 ♗e3 ♕c7 and ... 0-0-0 which is unclear but not so bad for Black. Harding suggests 11 ... ♕d7 12 ♖ad1 0-0-0, which looks fine to me, or perhaps ... h6 should be played first, to preserve the light-squared bishop from ♘g5) 10 ... ♗e6 11 0-0 and now Black, with pleasant development and a fine centre, opted to go on the offensive with 11 ... g5!? (of course, this has more point here than in the previous note as White has weakened his kingside) 12 ♘h2 h5 13 ♘e1 ♛b6 14 ♗e2 0-0-0 *(128)*

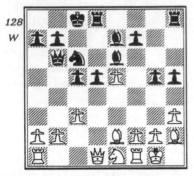

Geller – Campora, Moscow 1989, with exciting play. I would be very happy with Black here.

The English Grandmaster John Nunn tried **7 ♗b5+** recently against Wahls, Bundesliga 1988/9. Was it some sort of preparation? I don't know. The game went on: 7 ... c6 8 ♗d3 de 9 ♘xe5 ♘d7 10 ♘xd7 ♗xd7 11 ♛h5 ♗e6 12 0-0 ♛d5 and Black systematically exchanged all the pieces to make a draw. It is interesting that Nunn managed to get a lot less from the opening than he normally does with the white pieces in the Ruy Lopez. Instead of 7 ... c6, 7 ... ♗d7 8 ♗xd7+ (or 8 ♛e2 0-0) 8 ... ♘xd7 (also 8 ... ♛xd7, ... ♘c6) 9 ed (9 ♗f4 de=) 9 ... ♗xd6 10 ♛e2+ ♛e7 could be considered, which is absolutely level.

| 7 | ... | ♘c6 |

Pressurizing the e-pawn.

| 8 | ♛e2 | |

Other moves are also equal: 8 ed ♛xd6 9 0-0 ♗g4; or 8 ♗f4 0-0 9 0-0 de.

| 8 | ... | ♗e6 |

8 ... ♗g4!? is interesting: 9 ed ♛xd6 10 0-0-0 0-0-0 threatening ... ♘d4, ... ♗f6 or 10 ♗c3 0-0 11 0-0-0 ♛f4+ 12 ♔b1 ♗b4!∓.

| 9 | 0-0-0 | de |
| 10 | ♘xe5 | ♛d5! *(129)* |

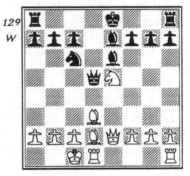

The point! It is useful to remember this manoeuvre, zeroing in on a2.

| 11 | ♘c4 | |

If 11 ♘xc6??, then not 11 ... ♛xc6?? 12 ♗b5+–, but 11 ... ♛xa2 menacing mate in one, which leaves White in big trouble e.g: 12 ♗c3? ♗g5+–+.

| 11 | ... | ♘d4 |

Can Black be more ambitious? Both 0-0 and 11 ... 0-0-0! 12 ♗c3 ♘d4 look fine to me.

| 12 | ♛e5 | ♛xe5 |
| 13 | ♘xe5 | 0-0 |

14 &c3 &f5
15 &he1 &c5
½-½

Klovan - Heuer, USSR 1962.

B2

5 ... &c5

Not such a strange move, as although Black is moving his only developed piece for the third time on successive moves, White will also have to waste time moving his queen's knight, as it impedes his queenside development.

6 &c4

If instead, 6 &b3 &e6 (a good blockading square, even if it has taken four moves to get there!) 7 &e3 &c6 8 &b5 (a game of Bronstein's against Bertok, USSR v Yugoslavia 1962, went *8 ed &xd6 9 &fd4 &cxd4 10 &xd4 0-0.* Black - Bronstein - is equal, but from this point on White's play beggars description. *11 &c4 &f6 12 c3 &xd4 13 &xd4 &e8+ 14 &f1? &f4 14 &c1 &h4 16 &d1 c5 17 &a4 &e4 18 f3 cd! 19 fe &f4+ 20 &g1 &e6! (130)*

130
W

21 &d1. 21 &xe6 &e3+ 22 &f1 fe and ... &f8+. *21 ....* *d3 22 &xd3 &c5+ 23 &d4 &c1+ 24 &f2 &xh1 0-1)* 8 ... &d7 9 &e2 &xe5 10 &xe5 de 11 0-0-0 c6 12 &c4 &c7 equal, Belov - Lein, USSR

1962. And moves such as 6 &c4?! d5 and 6 &e2 &c6 7 ed &xd6 are pleasant for Black.

6 ... d5
7 &g5

After 7 &e3 &e6 8 c4 dc 9 &xd8+ &xd8 10 &xc4, Neishtadt - Rojtman USSR 1955, 10 ... &c6 may also be a little better for White.

7 ... &d7

Again, this strange queen move, but this time it is forced as 7 ... &e7? 8 &xe7 &xe7 (8 ... &xe7 9 &e3 &e6 10 &d4 b6 11 &h4+ &e8 12 &f4 *(131)* cropped up in another of Bronstein's games, but this time he had White against Pyatnitsky, Kiev 1940. At this point Bronstein made the apt observation that if only Black could castle, he would have a good position! The game now terminated swiftly: 12 ... &e4 13 h4 &d7 14 &b5 &e7 15 0-0-0 1-0) 9 &xd5 snaffles a pawn, and 7 ... f6 8 ef gf 9 &fe5 is even

131
B

worse.

8 ♘e3   c6
9 ♘d4

9 ♗e2 ♘e7 10 0-0 Stan - Alexander, Corr 1950, is also a little better for White, but why not first 9 ... ♘e6 10 ♗h4 and then 10 ... ♘e7? For example: 11 ♗xe7 ♕xe7 12 0-0 ♘f4 with the intention of continuing ... 0-0, ... ♗e6 and ... ♘d7.

9 ...   ♘e6

For now, if 9 ... ♗e7 10 ♗xe7 ♕xe7 11 f4 with menacingly mobile e- and f-pawns. 11 ... f6? does not do because of 12 ♘f5.

10 ♗h4   ♕c7
11 ♗g3   ♕b6
12 ♘b3±

Bisguier - Guimard, Buenos Aires 1955.

Black's position is quite playable although he must beware of a possible charge of the white f-pawn.

Although objectively inferior to variation B1, variation B2 might appeal to those players who prefer a more closed position.

Of course, the best line (6 ♘c4) is far from obvious. and it is unlikely that one's opponent will find it over the board.

11) In Conclusion ...

This chapter is intended to tie up a few loose ends. The first part deals with those moves that have not been considered in the rest of the book and the second part is a brief description of move orders.

Part 1

Any player wishing to play Hanham's variation, will not only have to study chapters 8 and 9, but also chapters 1 and 10. In addition to this, on move 4, apart from ♘c3 and de, White can also play:

1	e4	e5
2	♘f3	d6
3	d4	♘f6
4	♘bd2	

4 ♗g5 h6 5 ♗h4 ♗e7=; or 4 ♘g5!? (this is a bit crude, the idea is 4 ... h6? 5 ♘xf7 ♔xf7 6 de with an attack) 4 ... ♗e7= (also 4 ... ed 5 ♗c4 d5=).

4	...	ed

As White's control over d4 is lessened, it seems natural to play a sort of Larsen's variation, but 4 ...

♘bd7 5 c3 ♗e7= is equally valid.

5	♘xd4	g6
6	♗d3	♗g7
7	c3	0-0
8	0-0	♖e8
9	f4	c5!?
10	♘4f3	♘c6

The game Zaitsev – Gusev, USSR 1969, continued: 11 ♖e1 d5!? 12 e5 ♘g4 13 ♘f1 ♕b6 14 ♗c2 c4+ 15 ♘e3 f6=.

And any player intending to play Antoshin's variation via the following move order:

1	e4	e5
2	♘f3	d6
3	d4	ed
4	♘xd4	♘f6

will have to know, not only chapter 6 (after 5 ♘c3) but also chapters 1 and 7. and:

5	♗d3!?	♗e7

5 ... g6 and ... ♗g7 is more aggresive.

6	c4	♘c6
7	♘xc6	bc
8	0-0	0-0
9	♘c3	♘d7
10	♗e3	♘e5
11	♗e2±	

Zaitsev – Antoshin, Sochi 1979.

Of course, both these possibilities are extremely rare, but you never know when you might have to play with Black against Zaitsev!

Finally, in this part, it is possible (but certainly not recommended) for Black to essay an early ... d5, 1 e4 e5 2 ♘f3 d6 3 d4 ed 4 ♘xd4 d5?! (also 4 ... ♘f6 5 ♘c3 d5?! 6 ed ♘xd5 7 ♘db5 ♘xc3 8 ♕xd8+ ♔xd8 9 ♘xc3 ♗f5 10 ♗g5+ f6 11 0-0-0+ ♘d7 12 ♗f4 Kondratiev – G. Petrosian, USSR 1971, but this ending is quite unpleasant for Black) 5 ed ♕xd5 6 ♗e3 (6 ♕e2+ ♗e7 7 ♘b5 ♘a6 8 ♘1c3±) 6 ... ♘f6 7 ♘c3 ♗b4 8 ♘db5 0-0! 9 ♘xc7 ♕a5 10 ♘xa8 ♗g4 11 ♗e2 ♖d8 12 0-0! *(132)* with wild complications, though favourable to White.

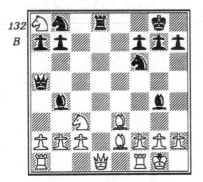

Kapengut-Kuzmin, USSR 1972.

Part 2

It is worth noting that the Philidor (particularly Hanham's variation) can be reached by several strange move orders, for instance: 1 d4 d6 2 e4 ♘f6 3 ♘c3 ♘bd7 4 ♘f3 e5 or 1 e4 d6 2 d4 e5!? 3 ♘f3 etc, as the ending after 3 de?! de ♕xd8+ ♔xd8 is nothing much for White.

After 1 e4 e5 the move 2 ♘f3 is the almost invariable choice for players of the white pieces, but, of course, it is necessary to learn a good defence against the alternatives, the King's Gambit, the Centre Game, the Danish Gambit etc.

It it possible to play 2 ... d6 against any of these? Yes, it is, but in general other moves are stronger. Some examples: 1 e4 e5 2 ♘c3 d6 3 ♗c4 ♘f6 4 d3 ♗e7 5 ♘ge2 0-0 6 0-0 c6 7 ♗b3 ♘bd7 8 h3 b5 9 f4± Kasper – Muller, East German Ch 1977: or 1 e4 e5 2 f4 d6?! 3 ♘c3 ♘f6 4 ♘f3 and now Nimzowitsch suggested 4 ... ♘bd7!?. And, in fact, the game Mestel – Georgadze in chapter 1, started 1 e4 e5 2 ♗c4 d6 and now 3 ♘f3 ♗e7 4 0-0 and so forth, but 3 f4 would have been more testing. Finally, I would like to wish all readers the best of luck with Philidor's Defence.

Index of Variations